Endorsements

"After painstaking research and personal implementation, David Taylor has pulled together three core components—personality, talents and values. Knowing what your specific personality style is, combined with your unique gifts and most important values, creates a potent mix that will serve you well in your career. The added bonus is that your personal and family life will be enriched, too. Follow his advice and you will undoubtedly reap the rewards."

- Les Hewitt
Co-author of the international bestseller, *The Power of Focus*
(www.thepoweroffocus.ca)

"Dave Taylor equips the 'equippers' through fresh, insightful, tried and tested leadership principles. 'Strength Zone' is a must-read for any person of influence who desires to make an investment in other peoples' lives."

- Ken Russell - Lead Pastor of Surrey Pentecostal Assembly

"We can have more than we've got because we can become more than we are. Use the principles taught in Strength Zone to become more than you already are!"

- Jim Rohn
The world's foremost business philosopher (www.jimrohn.com)

"Success in all aspects of your life, business and personal, comes from the actions you take in every situation. Strength Zone is the first book that simply and clearly defines exactly what those actions are for your situation and goals. Each person is different, but using this system you can't help but live a more successful and happy life."

- Don R. Campbell - Best-Selling Author, *Real Estate Investing in Canada*
(www.albertarein.com)

"In his book Dave shares his personal experiences, learnings, and readings which helps in developing focus for individuals who want to improve, learn and grow. You will be challenged to change, think, practice the principals, and be different. The opportunity exists for you to utilize the concepts in this book to be the best you can be, what more could you ask?"

- **R. A. (Dick) Molyneaux, P. Eng.** - Vice President of Operations SNC-Lavalin, T&D Calgary

"Every now and then a book comes along that can shake the train of your life off the old dull routine tracks of mundane living and onto a new exciting bold life filled with realized potential. David Taylor has written such a book! Sit back, grab this masterpiece and begin to watch your life transform!"

- **Ron White - Speaker, Author**
Ron White Training (www.memoryinamonth.com)

"Having spent many years as a career counselor, I have read and studied many different ways to help individuals explore and discover their personal career path. Dave has done a masterful job delineating and facilitating an understanding of and guidance through the key features of career development."

- **Dr. Randy Johnson, PHD** - Executive Director
Master's Counselling Service

"Your ability to identify your strengths and focus single-mindedly on doing what you do best is the key to great success, and 'Strength Zone' shows you how to do it."

- **Brian Tracy** - Author, *The Way To Wealth* (www.briantracy.com)

"I wish I had this book 35 years ago when I first started the business. Strength Zone is a no-nonsense manual on how to put together an effective, productive, harmonious group of people to run a project, corporation or a non-profit organization. This book is an excellent tool for anyone charged with such a responsibility!"

- **Ken Netzel** - Founder of Kenonic Controls

"It is said that experience is often the best teacher. Along with sound research, Dave Taylor threads his own experiences and insights into a framework of effectiveness that will help any individual or organization achieve the results they desire. 'Strength Zone' is a must read for anyone wanting to get the most out of life."

- **Merlyn Ness**
Director of Operations
Aetas Health

"Having used the DISC personality profiles in my wealth management business, the "Strength Zone" has provided me with a unique tool to add value for my clients. David's ability to synthesize leadership concepts with his practical life experience has resulted in a very readable and practical book that makes a great addition to a leaders library."

- **John Feldcher** - President
Wise Wealth Management

"Using the Strength Zone as a compass, it can lead one to a very fulfilling and satisfying career."

- **Anthony (Tony) Manning** - Vice President, Strategic Growth
Ber-Mac Electrical & Instrumentation
(www.Ber-Mac.com)

STRENGTH ZONE

By David M. Taylor

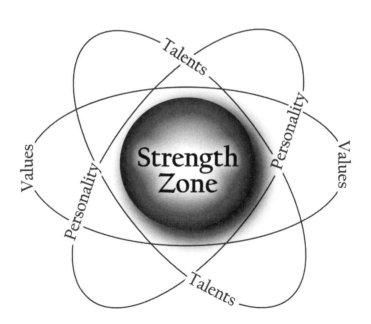

Library and Archives Canada Cataloguing in Publication

Taylor, David M., 1967-
Strength Zone: Discover your place of maximum
effectiveness / David M. Taylor.

ISBN 978-0-9781431-0-7

1. Self-actualization (Psychology) I. Title.

BF637.S4T393 2006 158.1 C2006-904905-X

First Printing 2006
Second Printing 2007

Publisher
Strength Zone Inc.
Calgary, Alberta, Canada
www.StrengthZone.ca

Project Manager
Debbie Elicksen, Freelance Communications, Calgary, Alberta

Design and Production
Bobbie-Jo Bergner, Mind's Design Studio, Calgary, Alberta

Printing
Friesen, Altona, Manitoba

Strength Zone - First Edition
Printed and Bound in Canada
Copyright 2006

Acknowledgements

This book represents an interesting journey I have been on over the last two years. It also describes the learning process I went through in the last ten years. Through this period, I have worked with many different clients on many projects, on a number of continents. I've worked with many people, been mentored by many, and hired and mentored many others. Through these experiences, I have discovered a number of extremely valuable principles that are not new, but unfortunately, are not well known. I hope this book communicates these principles to help everyone find and benefit from their Strength Zone.

I have relied on many people for their support and others for their expertise in order to get this book completed. First, I would like to thank my beautiful wife Kelly and kids Brittany, Lindsey, and Drew for their never-ending patience and support. They put up with me stealing valuable family time at home and on vacations, as the book was pieced together and as I continually subjected them to all kinds of profiles, tests, and exercises. I would especially like thank Lindsey for her illustrations that show up throughout this book.

I would like to thank Les Hewitt for his support and mentoring. It was Les that encouraged me to turn my manuscript into a book. He provided contacts and mentoring through this process.

Rod Chapman was instrumental in turning this into a book from a very early draft, which looked more like a project bid specification. Rod was recommended by Les as a top notch editor, and he certainly came through for me.

The following people read the manuscript and provided important feedback. I would like to thank them for their time and insights: Ramona DeRose, James Kishore, Dick Molyneaux, Barb Gandy, Brian Vogelaar, Kim Rans, Merlyn Ness, Ken Russell, and Lee Primeau.

I would like to thank The Institute for Motivational Living people – Deanna Walker – for her support and for allowing me to partner with Motivational Living to provide an online version of the DISC profile as part of this book.

Finally, Debbie Elicksen was invaluable in taking this book from an edited manuscript and turning it into a completed, published book.

Thanks to all these people for their time and effort in helping me achieve one of my goals by getting this book into production.

Table of Contents

Foreword

Think of the times in your life that made you wish for all the world that you had the power to make time stand still. Are they not moments of love, moments of joy? Simple moments of rest and quiet when all seems to be well. Something in your heart says, "Finally it has come. This is what I was made for!

- John Eldredge

No pleasure philosophy, no sensuality, no place nor power, no material success can for a moment give such inner satisfaction as the sense of living for a good purpose.

- Minot Simons

I enjoy spending time with people who continually strive to learn more and become more. David Taylor is an excellent example. Despite facing monumental challenges during a major work project, that many people would have succumbed to, he chose to learn from the experience. More impressively, he took dynamic action using new strategies he had learned and created a victory from something that looked impossible.

Because of this powerful proactive leadership style, he is well qualified to share his experiences with others who may be facing similar challenges.

Make no mistake, what you are about to learn is powerful. It will change the way you think and the way you approach your business. By focusing on your **Strength Zone**— which most people **don't** do—your confidence will grow and your energy will noticeably improve. In addition you will become more efficient, decisive, and productive.

I know these are big claims, however, I have the advantage of knowing that they work because they have worked for me for many years.

After painstaking research and personal implementation, David Taylor has pulled together three core components—personality, talents, and values. Knowing what your specific personality style is, combined with your unique gifts, and most important values, creates a potent mix that will serve you well in your career. The added bonus is that your personal and family life will be enriched, too. Follow his advice and you will undoubtedly reap the rewards.

- Les Hewitt
Co-author of the international bestseller, *The Power of Focus*

Introduction

There comes a special moment in everyone's life, a moment for which that person was born. That special opportunity, when he seizes it, will fulfill his mission – a mission for which he is uniquely qualified. In that moment, he finds greatness. It is his finest hour.

- Winston Churchill

The secret of success in life is for a person to be ready for opportunity when it comes.

- Benjamin Disraeli

How much do you love your job? Do you end each workday feeling fulfilled? Are you confident that you are in the right position with the right company? Are you focused on activities that matter to you? Are you capitalizing on your strengths? Are you effective and realizing your full potential? Are you having any fun?

For the majority of North Americans, the answer to these questions is a resounding "No!" Scholars and management gurus blame information overload, the pace of change, demands for instant service, downsizing, rightsizing, globalization, and our new knowledge-based economy. For whatever reason, far too many of us are feeling burned out, stressed out, tuned out, and turned off by the daily grind. We are living our lives in agonized mediocrity, desperately trying to avoid failure.

"Sometimes I hate this job so much I could just sit here and do it badly all day."

However, as this book will show, you can take simple, effective steps that will bring satisfaction in the work that you do. It *is* possible to end your day feeling satisfied with your efforts, knowing that you contributed and that your abilities were utilized. You can live your life confident enough to embrace failure by using what you learn from each failure as a steppingstone to success. You can break free from languishing in agonized mediocrity to enjoy a life flourishing in unimagined excellence.

Maybe you're not in the wrong job. Maybe you are just approaching work in a way that doesn't capitalize on your natural gifts.

Millions of people around the world could be substantially more effective, if only they could capitalize on their strengths. And if, after capitalizing on their strengths, these same people could truthfully identify their areas of weakness, they would discover how to multiply their effectiveness many times over. How? By teaming up with individuals who are strong in the areas where they are weak. We will discover how a person or a corporation can easily see a return on investment of well over 1,000 percent just by applying one aspect of the training provided in this book.

Many people get frustrated because they feel unable to discover and maximize their strengths. These people eventually burn out as they grow weary of struggling and give up the search. These are the people who seem ill-suited to their jobs. These are the people who turn up at work every day but who have, in effect, died and been buried years ago.

That is where I was headed when I was given a project to manage called Lilongwe. Managing the Lilongwe project to a successful outcome would prove to be the biggest challenge of my life to date. An offshore oil battery composed of two facilities – a drilling rig and a processing platform connected by a sub-surface umbilical cord – Lilongwe is located 140 kilometers off the coast of Angola in about 1,400 meters of water (the deepest of any other comparable installation). The processing platform is the largest of its kind ever built, and it produces 250,000 barrels of oil a day. Those conditions alone imposed huge design challenges.

At the time, I was a project manager at Kenonic Controls, the company that had won the bid for the automation portion of these facilities. We were responsible for installing the control system and the programming that allowed these facilities to safely and efficiently drill, produce, and ship oil. As an engineer for eleven years, I'd had my share of challenging problems to solve. I had even successfully managed a few small projects. But as my workload increased and my challenges grew bigger, I knew I had to become more effective or I'd never make it.

I was not ready for the Lilongwe project, in terms of my skill base. Moreover, after a thirteen-month assignment away, I asked if I could stick around home for a while before taking on another distant assignment. Unfortunately for me, the Y2K bubble had just burst and our company's work backlog was quite small. The CEO called me into his office and gave me a choice. I could take the project manager role on the Lilongwe project, which would mean leaving home for another twelve long months, or I could go home without pay to wait for the next project to come along. After talking it over with my wife, Kelly, I reluctantly decided to take on Lilongwe.

Typically, my projects had been small, requiring me to manage only about five people. Among the many challenges on the Lilongwe project was its sheer size. Lilongwe averaged about thirty people and spiked up to about one hundred. My project budgets had typically ran up to $1 million, but Lilongwe started at more than $15 million. With about 100,000 man-hours anticipated over a twelve-month period, this was the largest Lump Sum Turn Key (LSTK) project in our company's history. Kenonic Controls did not have a profitable history with LSTK projects, and I had no experience whatsoever managing this type of project. This was also the first global offshore LSTK project that I had managed.

And it was truly global. We worked in Canada, United States, Holland, Korea, Angola, Norway, India, Germany, and the United Kingdom. We had people in our Calgary office from Canada, U.S., India, Angola, Germany, Bosnia, El Salvador, and Pakistan. We had no tracking systems for materials management, finances, or employee hours. We were using new technology that no one in our office was familiar with, and in some cases, the technology was not even developed. Due to the global aspect of the project, we had to use the Internet for document sharing and for concurrent engineering. We had an extremely compressed schedule. We had inaccurate and changing engineering data (and, in some cases, no data at all) from the other contracted companies. And, to top it all off, Kenonic had just been purchased by a major U.S. conglomerate and this was our first major project within the new company. Our new owners had different project management and financial reporting standards that we needed to learn. Then September 11 happened, instantly changing the face of world travel and making it substantially more difficult to obtain work visas in many of the countries we were working in.

I would love to be able to say that despite all of these challenges, we experienced no failures, but if that were the case, I wouldn't have learned anything. I would not have written this book. Some of our early failures included:

- We issued purchase orders too quickly (at the prompting of our new owners) so that division financial statements would benefit. This resulted in problems later on, as we established contracts and bills of material that were different from the purchase orders that we issued.

- I brought people onto the project from other divisions of the company based solely on internal recommendations. I never interviewed these people, assuming that the recommendations were made by people with my best interests at heart. Some of these new hires turned out to be quite damaging to our project (and to the company) and subsequently had to be removed.

- In one case, I placed people of one nationality as team leads over a group of a different nationality. Based on contracts, location, technical strength, and capability, this was the correct decision. Based on the history over the last century or two between these nationalities, this was an extremely poor decision, one that negatively affected the project.

- I compressed too large a workload onto too few people.

- I allowed some subcontractors to freewheel and didn't provide proper controls until they started sending me change notices.

- I did not always handle personality conflicts properly or promptly, which resulted in additional problems.

- I placed some people in the wrong roles, and consequently did not get the quality and quantity of work that I expected.

However, from each failure I tried to learn a lesson and to pass the lesson I learned onto my team. Largely due to this approach, I think, the Lilongwe project turned into a monumental success. We completed the project on time, with almost twice the estimated gross profit. We trained a huge technical staff, starting with two managers and ending with fifty fully trained technical people. We increased our project budget from $15.6 million to $28 million due to additional scope requested by our client. Our client was very happy with our performance and continued to give us work from other contractors, who were failing in their roles. Due to our performance on Lilongwe, we were given ten additional projects of similar size, totaling over $100 million. In short, Lilongwe was a phenomenal success.

On a personal front, as a result of Lilongwe, I moved from managing one large project, to managing multiple large projects, to managing multiple large projects while also managing human resources and recruiting, to a position as vice president of my business unit.

So how did this huge challenge, with many up-front failures and an ill-equipped engineer at the helm, become one of the most successful projects in Kenonic's history?

Turning point #1

None of this would have been possible if I had not spent some time studying, reading, and attending seminars. These activities led me to a seminar entitled *The Power of Focus* (refer to Appendix B: Recommended Resources) by Les Hewitt, a top business and personal development coach. Listening to Hewitt was an awakening for me. I took copious notes, bought his book, and implemented many of the practices that he encourages, such as:

- Establishing clearly defined and measurable goals with a defined timeline

- Working toward the realization of these goals

- Ensuring a balance in all areas of my life

At this point, I was working up to eighty hours a week on the Lilongwe project, trying to keep my head above water. Hewitt's advice helped me focus and become much more efficient and effective. My average workload fell back to about fifty hours a week. I then began to give seminars to my team members on these principles, and the change was amazing. They, too, began to get much more efficient and effective. This gave our project a huge boost.

However great the change with turning point #1, I soon realized that something was missing. Leadership skills were at the top of this list – skills that were absolutely required to run a project of this magnitude. This became apparent as I began running into situations that I was not handling effectively. For example:

- There was conflict internally between team members, and externally between team members and vendors.

- My influence with others was not always positive, or the results were not positive.

- I was too demanding, not looking for a win-win situation.

- I had trouble setting a proper course of action for our team.

- I didn't realize that leadership is sometimes about being a follower, especially when others on the team are more qualified in certain areas.

- After successfully concluding one phase of the project, I was happy just to push on to the next challenge, as opposed to celebrating milestone victories with the team and creating positive momentum.

Turning point #2

Enter John C. Maxwell. I discovered Maxwell's books at Chapters one evening as I waited for my kids to get out of one of their weekly Tuesday night activities. I was browsing through the leadership section and saw *The 21 Irrefutable Laws of Leadership*. I picked it up, breezed through the first couple of pages, and became hooked. Over the next few months, I read this book and many others written by Maxwell. I signed up for his monthly mentorship program, and I attended a number of the seminars he sponsored. Through all of this, I began to develop as a leader. I also started to run seminars on leadership for my team and took some of the members to seminars. Again, the growth I saw in the people around me was nothing short of amazing.

This began an explosion in personal growth in my life that continues today. I have read books and attended seminars from many well-respected authors and leaders, including John C. Maxwell, Les Hewitt, Peter Drucker, Zig Ziglar, Michael Aarons, Jim Collins, Ken Blanchard, Jack Welch, Rudy Giuliani, Marcus Buckingham, Bill Hybels, Steven Sample, Tim Sanders, T.D. Jakes, Brian Tracy, Jim Rohn, and many others. Refer to Appendix A for a list of recommended reading (note that this list is available for download from www.StrengthZone.ca).

Of this list, the teachings of Les Hewitt and John C. Maxwell have had the most incredible impact on my life. Without their input, I would still be struggling fruitlessly, working more than fifty hours a week trying to keep my head above water.

However, there was still something missing. According to Maxwell's *Law of the Lid*, I needed to raise my level of effectiveness by understanding my own strengths and weaknesses along with the strengths and weaknesses of the members of my team. I was continually putting myself, and others, into roles as they came up – as opposed to trying to define the role and placing the most-qualified or best-fitting person into it. As you can imagine, this resulted in a lot of inefficiencies, a number of spectacular failures, and some hard feelings.

Turning point #3

Turning point #3 happened when I discovered the benefits of personality profiling. I learned about this technique through some friends who were talking about Myers Briggs testing. Then my employer's human resource (HR) group conducted a seminar on DISC personality profiling. From this, I realized I had some weaknesses, but I also had some dominant strengths. I learned that I was a high D, which is basically a bulldozer type of personality. Although this didn't sound good at the time, it was a start. I was beginning to identify my strengths and was now becoming aware of my weaknesses. The DISC profile taught me how to deal with my weaknesses and how to use my strengths to become more effective. I began to understand what made other people tick and how people with different personality types needed to be dealt with to allow them to be efficient, effective, and happy in their role. This was excellent. I was starting to head in the right direction. I was focused. I was developing as a leader, and now, through a simple system of personality profiles, I was beginning to understand how to deal with others more effectively.

Looking back, I had come a long way already. Here's an example, drawn from my past experience. While still a junior engineer at Kenonic Controls, I was in charge of the automation work on a gas plant project for a client in northern Canada. We were doing all of the design, engineering, and testing in a large warehouse in Calgary, and due to the aggressive schedule, we had a day shift and a night shift. We all worked long hours striving to meet the deadlines, causing some stress with the engineering and design team, as well as with the client.

The client's project manager was in a cost-saving mode and looking for the cheapest way possible to ship the automation equipment to the site. However, he failed to inform the trucking company that automation equipment needs to be shipped in a climate-controlled, air-ride environment. When the trucking company showed up at our warehouse with a flat-bed truck, ready to move our sensitive automation equipment 800 kilometers north, fully exposed to rain and snow, I pulled the truck driver and his crew aside and stated in no uncertain terms that they were not taking any of our equipment on that truck. Although I did explain my reasoning, I did not tailor the message to anyone's personality style, as I later learned how to do, and as a result, the driver and his crew left in a poor state of mind.

When the driver arrived back at the warehouse with the proper truck, he was still in a foul mood, raising his voice and even yelling at me for some alleged inconsistency in the paperwork. Due to my inexperience and my lack of knowledge about how to read personalities, I responded in like fashion. This, of course, only made the situation worse. Eventually, the dust settled. The equipment was loaded, and we all went our separate ways, each side angry and convinced that the other person was an idiot, or worse.

Although the equipment eventually made it to the site in operating condition, I knew I had failed to interact with the driver in a professional and courteous fashion. This incident stayed with me. I knew I had to find some way to get better at interacting with others, or I would struggle in my career.

Contrast this incident with one that happened recently. One of our vendors called in a poor mood to say that his invoice had not been paid. It just happened that the program manager for this project was in my office at the time of the call. I put the phone on speaker so that we could work through the issue together. However, the abrupt and abrasive attitude of the vendor caused the program manager, who could also be abrupt and abrasive, to explode in a frenzy of words, expletives, and threats.

I realized from my DISC personality training that the vendor, as well as the project manager, were both D personalities. Therefore, I tailored my response to D personalities. I knew that, among other things, Ds want immediate results. They also want to take control of situations. I entered the fray by asking a couple of simple questions. "Why was the invoice issued? Have the contractual milestones been reached, met, and signed off by all appropriate parties?" This allowed the vendor to talk and maintain control of the situation. It also allowed me to lead him to a solution without actually spelling it out for him.

The answer to the first question was, "The invoice was issued because we want to get paid." This made sense, but it wasn't according to the contract. The answer to the second question was no. I began to realize that the vendor didn't necessarily want his invoice paid immediately, although that is what he was asking for. He was really wondering *how* he could get it paid, and in what timeframe. By leading the vendor through the process, and explaining what he needed to do to get the invoice paid, we established a realistic timeline for the payment.

Unlike the incident with the trucker, this time both parties left feeling good about themselves and what they had accomplished. In the intervening years between these two incidents, I had learned how to work within my Strength Zone and to read the zones of others. I was also starting to see great results in my team, as they too began to see the benefits of increasing their proficiency in these areas.

Back before I had taken DISC training, I had a problem with being highly impatient – a classic problem for a high D like me. D personalities typically want to get to the point as soon as possible. If they want more detail about something, they will ask for it. When people would come to me with situations or issues or even just to explain a story, I would require the whole scenario to be spelled out in a few sentences or less.

Unfortunately, this behavior did not buy me any points with the people I was dealing with. The high I personalities wanted to tell me about all kinds of history and interpersonal interactions that I was not interested in, and people who were high C types wanted to give me much more detail than I cared to hear. For example, one day when I asked my wife if she was able to get the shoes she had headed out to buy that morning, I was looking for a yes or no answer. However, she proceeded to give me a ten-minute reply that included a month's worth of proceedings before the purchase transaction, as well as a bunch of detail around a number of totally irrelevant and unrelated events. I made the classic mistake of asking her to get to the point, and consequently, I had to suffer the consequences of my rudeness.

Now, since I have begun to use what I have learned from personality profiles, this has changed dramatically. I now understand that it isn't about me, or what I want, or how I want information to be delivered to me. It is all about how I can communicate best with others by observing *their* personality styles and by adjusting my approach to make our interaction as efficient and effective as possible. People who have high I and high C personalities need to sit and talk through things differently than do D or S types. I've realized that this interaction makes them self-assured, confident, and effective. By taking the small talk away, I leave them feeling frustrated and demoralized. Don't get me wrong – there is a time for brevity and abruptness. However, it is not all the time. Having said that, it is also important to note that I am far from perfect (as my wife will attest), and I still make many mistakes. The difference is that in the post-mistake analysis, I can now usually pick out where I went wrong and make a mental note to improve in the future.

But I soon realized that knowing about personality types wasn't all I needed. I was still running into issues with my team members, even though I was now dealing much more effectively with them. Issues were coming up that I hadn't counted on, something that went much deeper than lack of leadership skills or personality clashes. Each individual seemed to have some ideals that they did not want to compromise. These ideals did not always fall into alignment with the ideals of the corporation or with the ideals of their fellow team members.

Turning point #4

I thought I understood my values. I thought I knew what I valued most, and least, in life. But I never really thought that values should be considered in conjunction with personality profiles until I began studying some conflict management techniques using two sources: the Center for Creative Leadership Conflict Management Series and a John C. Maxwell seminar on values.

The conflict management training showed that the most common cause of conflict is between personality and values. This is not hard to believe. It has been proven throughout history. However, what the conflict management courses did not teach was that personality and values combine into areas of strength or areas of contention, depending on the situation. For example, a person who has a detail-oriented personality probably also values quality as opposed to quantity. Placing this person into an area of mass production, instead of detailed design or quality assurance, may result in fireworks (I'm speaking from experience here. I definitely experienced this after placing a few of these people in the wrong positions). I began to sense that there is a link between strengths, personality, and values.

However, as you might have guessed, I was still coming up short. There was still something missing. There still seemed to be a gap in the process of helping a person determine his or her true strengths. I began to realize that understanding personality and defining values is only part of the process. Knowing these things allows a person to become more effective and efficient – both individually and as part of a team – but it seems to come up short in determining strengths. For example, I wondered why some people seem to be able to thrive in a creative environment, where everything has to be created from scratch, while others hate this environment and would rather build on pre-existing structures. It does not seem to have anything to do with values or personality. Why do some people excel in a competitive environment, while competition turns others off? I began to think that creativity and competition appear to be better defined as talents, as opposed to personality or values, although they all seemed to be related.

Turning point #5

What am I truly gifted at? I realized this question needed definition. Only then would I be able to focus on my areas of talent, regardless of the role I happened to be in at the time. I am not talking about basic competencies as defined by the typical performance evaluations that we see in most corporations. Although well intentioned, these competency-based evaluations are ineffective because they force everyone into specific molds requiring specific skills. A better solution is to define the requirements of each role and the expected outcomes. In my case, I needed to determine how I could best apply my talents to reach, or exceed, the desired outcome. I didn't want to concentrate on making a weak skill set better; I wanted to concentrate on making a strong talent stronger and on applying this talent successfully to achieve my desired outcome.

Finally, by looking at the overlap or commonality in the strengths as defined by my values, personality and talents, I found that I could start building my skills and knowledge to become stronger and even more effective in the role that I happened to be in.

This is exactly what I did, and the change in my personal effectiveness and work satisfaction was phenomenal. As I shared these techniques with my team members, they too began experiencing huge boosts in effectiveness, both at work and at home. They also began to advance from their current work roles into more senior and more complex roles. Although I didn't know it at the time, I was discovering my Strength Zone.

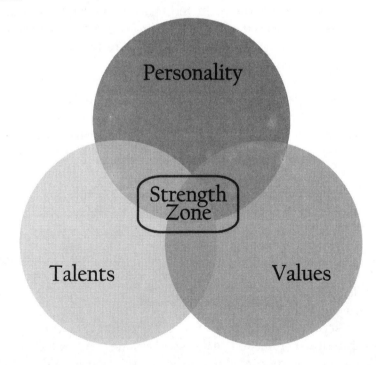

The first step in becoming a more effective person is to define your Strength Zone. But how do you find it? I have struggled with this question for some time. After reading a great many books dealing with business, leadership, and self-improvement, I have been frustrated by the lack of detail provided in this important area. All of the books I read talked about how important it is to find and work in areas of strength. Some of these books have talked about identifying areas of excellence, but they go no further than saying you need to find these areas. Other books talk about the benefits of finding the one thing that you can be best in the world at, but they stop short of defining this on an individual level.

This book will help you discover your own Strength Zone. The process starts with identifying your values. You'll learn how your values can mesh – or clash – with the people close to you, and even with your corporation. You'll gain tremendous insights into your personality type – how it shapes you, how it determines your strengths and weaknesses, and how it is absolutely critical that you find the environment you need to be most effective. This book will show you how to examine your talents to discover what you are truly gifted at and how to apply those talents to any role. Most important, you'll discover how to align your values with your personality and talents. When you do that, you will be operating full time in your Strength Zone and on your way to enjoying a life flourishing in unimagined excellence!

———————

Getting the most out of this book

To get the most out of this book, you must:

1.   Develop a desire to understand and master the concepts.

2.   Spend time reading, researching, and practicing the concepts.

3.   Take time as you are reading to make notes and jot down thoughts about where you can improve.

4.   Get together with others and discuss aspects of the book.

5.   Practice dealing with different personality types in different situations.

6.   Apply these principles every chance you get.

7.   Ensure that you complete all the exercises and answer all the questions.

8.   Spend time redefining your roles to take advantage of what you have learned.

9.   Work within these redefined roles, continually striving to be as effective as possible.

10. Visit the web site for activities, downloads, and information each time you see one of the following symbols:

 This symbol indicates that there are activities that need to be completed. These activities are outlined in your book and you can download the activity sheets from or use the online tools provided at www.StrengthZone.ca.

 This symbol indicates that there are activity sheets, forms or other information available for download at www.StrengthZone.ca

 This symbol indicates that there is more information located at www.StrengthZone.ca

www.StrengthZone.ca

To get the activities and book-related downloads, you must first register as a user at www.StrengthZone.ca. This is done by selecting the "Register" link on the top right hand side of the screen. Enter the required information and select the "Register" button at the bottom of the resultant screen to submit. A "Member's Zone" menu will now become available to you. In order for you to get access to all of the material, you must register your copy of Strength Zone. This can be done by selecting the "Member's Zone" menu item, then the "Member resources," and finally "DISC Profile" and, when prompted, enter the unique code printed on the back inside cover of the book.

After you have completed this process, you can access all areas and features that the site offers. When signing onto the site in the future, you will only have to log on by selecting the "Login" link on the top left hand corner of www.StrengthZone.ca and all the features of the site will be available to you.

If you purchase the PDF version of the book, the unique code entry process is not required. This is automated at the time of purchase.

Your Strength Zone

· 1 ·

Of all the responsibilities you face in life, this is one of the most important: to identify that area of excellence that can have the greatest positive impact on your career and your income. Once you know what that is, pour all your energies into becoming the best you can possibly be in that key area.

- TurboCoach by Brian Tracy and Campbell Fraser

Know thy audience: to exceed expectations, you must understand personality types and character identities, and how to uncover them.

- Life is a Series of Presentations by Tony Jeary

If you do not fully understand your strengths, you are not being fully effective – you are selling yourself short. You are not living up to your potential with your spouse, kids, co-workers, boss, or business partners. Imagine being twice as effective as you are now. What about five or ten times more effective? It is absolutely possible!

What's holding you back? The first step in becoming more effective is to define your strengths and to know your Strength Zone. If you are not working in your Strength Zone, what possibilities are eluding you? Just define your strengths and use them to your advantage. It's that simple.

Once you have determined your personal Strength Zone, what about helping others find their own Strength Zone? This one thing will do more to multiply your effectiveness and efficiency than anything else. When you personally become more efficient and effective because you are working in your Strength Zone, you will have reached your peak – unless you share this knowledge with those around you, helping them find and work within their own Strength Zone. You can then encourage the people who have strengths where you have weaknesses to move into your weak areas, thus making the team stronger.

Consider the following diagram. The vertical axis illustrates your potential in terms of your Strength Zone, which is the combination of your values, personality, and talents. The horizontal axis indicates your technical competency in the area of your vocation. The area of the graph indicates your effectiveness in your current role.

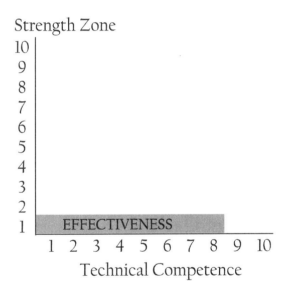

Many people struggle to raise their technical competency from an eight (if they are lucky enough to be that high) to a ten. This struggle follows the 80/20 rule (also called Paretto's Principle) that it takes twenty percent of the effort to get to eighty percent competency, but it takes eighty percent of the effort to go the last twenty percent to full competency. And what does all this extra effort buy you? Only a two-eighths, or twenty-five percent, increase in competency.

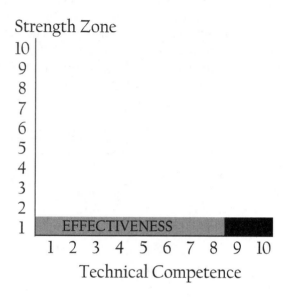

Now, what if you could make a few changes in how you handle yourself, your work, and your interaction with others, and with very little effort, see a one hundred percent increase in your effectiveness?

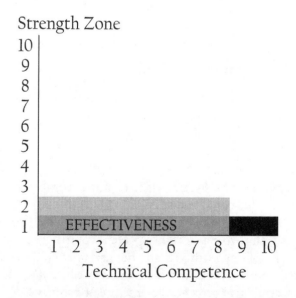

Amazingly, this is absolutely possible – if you can learn how to work within your Strength Zone. If you learn to leverage your values, personality, and talents in your everyday life and work, you can easily become, at a minimum, one hundred percent more effective, as illustrated in the graph above. Moreover, this increase in effectiveness can be realized with little effort on your part. Certainly, it takes substantially less effort than it takes to move from a technical competency level of an eight to a level ten.

"Oh, not bad. The light comes on, I press the bar, they write me a check. How about you?"

This leads us into a brief discussion on leadership. Everyone, whether working in an official leadership position or working in the trenches, is a leader in some aspect of life. For example, you might be a leader at home, at church, with your children or in an organization or association you have joined. Your effectiveness in these areas will be limited by your knowledge of, and willingness to work in, your Strength Zone.

It has been said that that leadership is influence, nothing more and nothing less. However, before you can influence others to follow, you must understand yourself. You must define your Strength Zone – your area of strength. If you don't identify your strengths and weaknesses, you cannot understand your Strength Zone, and therefore, you cannot influence others effectively. Your leadership ability and your effectiveness as a person will be compromised. The same holds true for understanding others. If you do not understand others, if you cannot help others identify their Strength Zone and work within it, you will not have as much of a positive influence on them. Therefore, your leadership ability and your effectiveness as a person will be compromised. This applies equally to leaders and to those who don't consider themselves to be leaders.

Peter Drucker states that individuals must determine what it is that they do best, and then continue to exploit these strengths. He goes on to say that if North American countries are going to compete in the world economy in the future, we have to become effective and efficient. Failure to do this will result in substandard corporations. If this happens, we will be outperformed by corporations in other countries. We will cease to exist as powerful and monetarily influential nations. This has been corroborated by numerous other studies and people, including the study *No Monopoly on Creativity* by Richard Florida and the book *Unlimited Wealth* by Paul Zane Pilzer.

How do we ensure that this happens? We have to ensure we place ourselves, and other people around us, in their Strength Zone. We must use this strategy to build strong, creative business environments. Failure to do so will result in a less effective, less efficient, and less creative work force. Eventually, it will result in the fall of North America from being a world economic power.

I have seen what happens when people do not concentrate on their strengths. Most people end up stuck in, what I call, the Doom Loop (as illustrated in the following diagram). In this self-destructive loop, people desire to be successful but they do not understand where their strengths are and therefore do not know how they can be successful. They start out with great attitudes and attempt to do everything they are asked to do, but because they do not understand their own strengths and weaknesses, they will soon experience frustration and failure. This leads them to attempt a restart in their life and/or career by moving to a different role or a new job/career. However, they still haven't determined their strengths and weaknesses, so they will inevitably end up exactly in the same frustrated and failing position as they just left.

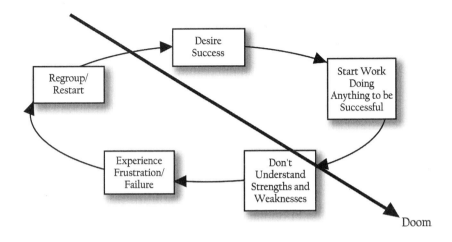

What living in your Strength Zone provides is a process for individuals to follow that helps them determine where their major strengths lie and then how to take the knowledge of these strengths and apply it to either redefine their current role(s) or redefine how they would approach their role in the most effective and efficient method possible. These strength areas, called Strength Zones, are a combination of Values, Personality, and Talents.

As illustrated in the Success Loop shown below, these Strength Zones allow an individual to adapt their new role or position in a way that allows them to take advantage of their well defined strengths and to fulfill the role successfully. As they continue to work in this role, they will monitor their progress through the use of feedback and will adapt their approach to the role based on the application of this feedback and the knowledge of their Strength Zone. As in the Doom Loop, a person that is operating in the Success Loop will also move into new roles. However, they are moving into these new roles based on the success in their current role, not because they are being moved due to failure.

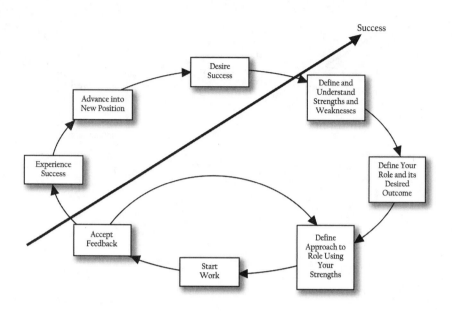

I experienced the Doom Loop firsthand at the start of the Lilongwe project, when I was working so hard to just keep my head above water. I was doing many tasks that needed to be done, but that did not need to be done by me. For example, I hated completing schedules and doing the detailed work around cost reporting. I was vitally interested in looking at the results and making project steering decisions based on the biweekly reports, but I was not interested in getting bogged down in the details of producing the reports. Yet, I continued to do it because I did not realize that this task was not in my Strength Zone.

As I began to work my way through the Strength Zone process, I realized I should begin to find others to complete the tasks that were not taking advantage of my strengths and were bogging me down. The first task I chose to shed was project reporting. I made two immediate changes:

1.   I hired a cost controller/scheduler who loved doing cost reports and schedules. This person was great at this task and took pleasure in this activity.

2.   I hired a consultant to come in and write a few pieces of code that automated some of the more monotonous aspects of the reporting process.

In doing this, I was able to free up more of my time for the things I was really good at and enjoyed doing, which moved me closer to my Strength Zone. This is part of the Success Loop process; define your role and your approach to that role to utilize your strengths.

In making these simple changes, I was able to place someone else into their Strength Zone as a cost controller/scheduler. This person was truly gifted in these areas and liked to do this type of work. The resulting reporting, cost control, and scheduling activities were never so easy and error-free.

I have also seen countless inefficiencies on projects, where people were picked for a role because they were available at the time, as opposed to being qualified for the role or, stated more clearly, they were an available warm bum in a seat but not necessarily strong in the areas required to be successful for the role. This inevitably results in:

- Frustrated individuals who feel trapped in a role that does not suit their strengths. They begin to question their self-worth, and their self-confidence can be damaged.

- Frustrated team members who feel the mismatched individual is failing the team.

- Frustrated project managers who begin to see the whole project team stressed due to the misplacement of one individual.

I recently experienced this myself, as I moved from an operations management role into a vice president role. As the operations manager, I was responsible for, among many things, interviewing, hiring, and general resource management within a business unit. As you can imagine, this is a challenging and time-consuming role, not to mention thankless. You can never hire fast enough. Or you have hired too fast and have not supplied a properly qualified individual. Needless to say, I did not really enjoy the role. I found it kind of draining. When I moved from the operations management role to role of vice president of the same business unit, I didn't select anyone to step into the operations management position. Where it made sense, I was able to move most of the other responsibilities to others, but when it came to the resource side of the operations role, no one was available, interested, or qualified.

This caused me no end of frustration. I was not able to step up and dig into the VP role properly, and I was not doing a great job on the resource management side due to lack of interest and time. On the way home from work one evening, I decided to fully define the role(s) that I was trying to hand off and determine the strength areas required for someone to successfully fill these role(s). I was moving from the Doom Loop to the Success Loop.

At work the next day, I mapped out the current position with all of its responsibilities and requirements. I then looked within my business unit to see who had the required skill sets and strengths. I divided the position into three separate and distinct roles and redefined the position in terms of responsibilities and required strengths. Then I approached the selected candidates. As soon as these candidates saw that they would not have to take on the complete role, and that the new role matched their strengths and was only part time, they were happy to take on the new positions. And I was more than happy to give my former job to them.

As mentioned previously in this chapter, people that are frustrated in a role because they are not using their strengths properly begin to question their self-worth. This is another aspect of the Doom Loop. Fred Smith, in the articles on his website _www.BreakfastWithFred.com_, states, "People who are clear on their self-worth see life as a challenge; those who are foggy see it as a threat." How can you be more productive and effective – by seeing life as a challenge or by seeing life as a threat?

Assuming you answered, "by seeing life as a challenge," how can you become clear on your self-worth? You must understand your strengths and your weaknesses. If you know what your strengths and weaknesses are, and you build a plan to exploit your strengths, it will give you confidence in all areas of your life. Fred Smith goes on to say, "Leadership means understanding people, identifying a system for measuring, and finding the right fit. Recognizing patterns of behavior enables us to create a state of higher productivity." This is my point exactly. We must understand ourselves and understand others. We must use this understanding to place ourselves and other people into the roles and situations that make them the most productive. We must strive to work in the Success Loop.

Some real life examples of people living in the Success Loop are illustrated in Table 3.1 of *The Millionaire Mind*. Author Thomas J. Stanley indicates that eighty-six percent of millionaires in North America today have developed an appreciation of their interests and abilities, and that eighty-eight percent have realized how to make accurate judgments about people. The millionaires included in this study were not sports superstars, dot-com wonders, or Hollywood divas. The study subjects were typically first-generation millionaires living in middle-class neighborhoods and leading family-oriented, well-balanced lives. What are these statistics showing? They are showing that these millionaires, arguably the most successful people in North America, have discovered how to be effective and efficient by understanding their own strengths, along with the strengths of those around them. This has also been proven in corporate cultures as was illustrated in the studies completed and summarized into the book *Good to Great* by Jim Collins.

So, how do you work most effectively and efficiently? In which types of work environments are you:

- Most productive?
- Least productive?
- Happy?
- Unhappy?
- Stressed?
- Not stressed?

Why are you this way in these different environments? In what ways do you influence others? Are you a positive influence or a negative influence?

My point is that for YOU to be the best YOU can be, as a person or as a leader, you must first understand yourself. You MUST know what your strengths and weaknesses are and then you MUST actively strive to define and redefine your roles in life to continually take advantage of your strengths. You MUST endeavor to remove yourself from the pitfalls of the Doom Loop and move to and live in the Success Loop.

Once you have got your strengths working for you, then you need to help those around you. In order to be really effective as an individual or as a leader, you must be able to help others capitalize on their strengths. How can you do this? How can you motivate others? There have been many studies done and books written that show leaders must, among other things, provide interesting and challenging work for their team members. But how can you provide interesting and challenging work if you cannot help your team members determine their strengths, especially if you cannot even determine your own strengths? We will work through a process that will help you discover your Strength Zone. You can help others apply this same process to discover their Strength Zone. Use this information to help those around you and to place others in the areas of their strengths.

Keep in mind that you must not use people selfishly to achieve something for yourself. You need to build relationships with people. These relationships form the foundation for success. Every goal you are trying to achieve and every outcome that you are searching for will be successful only if your interactions with others along the way are successful. You need to try hard to understand the individuals with whom you are working. Then use this knowledge to ensure that you provide both customized and maximized service for each individual. This not only maximizes the effectiveness of the individual, it maximizes the effectiveness of you and all those people with whom the individual interacts. When you are working in your strength areas and you have helped those around you to work in their strength areas then you are truly working in your Strength Zone.

You can only rise in influence and effectiveness to a certain level, and you will stay at that level unless you are willing to learn and grow as an individual. You cannot lead people any higher than you are able to grow yourself. If you don't understand your Strength Zone, you will not be able to grow to your highest level. As mentioned before, this does not just apply to individuals in official leadership positions. This applies to everyone, including you, no matter what your role is in everyday life. Everyone needs to strive to become more efficient and effective by defining and working in his or her own Strength Zone.

John C. Maxwell is a real-life example of someone who has followed these principles. After starting his career as an ordained minister in a small town in Indiana, within a few years, the church for which he was responsible grew from an attendance of two (he and his wife) to several hundred. Maxwell soon realized that he was not working in his Strength Zone, but as he moved on to larger churches he continued refining his strengths and striving to work in those areas. His disciplined approach allowed him to become extremely effective and efficient. He has now founded at least three companies directed at leadership development, along with a non-profit organization dedicated to training a million leaders worldwide. He has written over thirty books and sold more than seven million copies, including *The 21 Irrefutable Laws of Leadership*, a New York Times bestseller with over one million copies sold. He speaks to more than 350,000 people every year, and he is now known as North America's foremost expert on leadership.

Maxwell became aware of his strengths (communication, networking, leading, and creating) and he chose to focus on these strengths instead of trying to better his weaknesses. He built his life and his business around these strengths, and his accomplishments have excelled beyond the wildest dreams of most people.

Maxwell is not alone in this achievement. Many other people who have achieved significant success have also followed this pattern: Warren Buffett, Bill Gates, Mother Theresa, and Michael Dell, to name just a few.

Maxwell realized that he performed best in the areas of communication, networking, creating, and leading, so he concentrated his efforts in these areas. He applied all of these strengths in the area of leadership, and his results have been outstanding.

To illustrate how this can apply to you, consider a situation where you are enrolled in university and training to be an engineer. You have the following qualities:

- You love challenges
- You love to learn
- You are driven by a need to achieve
- You love to meet and interact with people
- You are accurate, efficient, and effective

- You are responsible and a person of integrity

These are all qualities that managers love to see in engineers. It appears as if you have chosen the correct career. There is only one problem. As you are coming to the end of your last work term and the thrill of learning new things and moving from university to the work force is wearing off, you begin to realize that you hate the monotony of the detailed work required of an engineer. Being stuck in a cubicle away from people for what seems like days on end is sapping your strength. You find it totally de-motivating. It feels like you are going to suffocate before the day is over.

What are you going to do?

Some options for you to choose from are listed below. Some of these options will appeal to you more than others. Your choices may not line up with the choices of your co-workers, spouse, or friends, but none of the options are wrong – unless you pick one that does not fit with your personal values, personality, or talents. Even then, it is not wrong; it is only less efficient for you and potentially limiting to you as a person and as a leader.

Options:
- Quit engineering and go back to university to take something else

- Continue with engineering, put up with your feelings, and collect your paycheck every two weeks

- Continue with engineering but move into a sales role or a business development role where you can use your technical expertise and be out dealing with people and clients on a daily basis

Which option best fits what you would do? Why would you choose this option over the others?

What you have to realize is the description of you provided earlier is not exclusive to personality, talents, or values. Values, talents, and personality will be further defined later in this book. For now, values can be defined as your concept of what is right or worthwhile. Talents are your special natural abilities, and personality is your temperament.

The list of qualities of the engineer in the example above is composed of values, personality, and talents. There is crossover between all of these qualities. Loving a challenge, for example, can be a talent as well as a personality trait – and it can even be a value.

The important thing to realize is that your values, personality, and talents cannot be considered in isolation from each other. In trying to define your Strength Zone so that you can build yourself into a better person and become a better leader, you have to consider all three of these areas and understand how they interact uniquely to form the entity that is you. Tony Jeary makes this point in his book *Life is a Series of Presentations*, where he states, "Know thy audience: to exceed expectations, you must understand personality types, character identities and how to uncover them." This is what the rest of this book will attempt to do. Identify your values, personality profile, and talents, and then use this information to determine your Strength Zone.

In *TurboCoach*, authors Brian Tracy and Campbell Fraser state, "Of all the responsibilities you face in life, this is one of the most important: to identify that area of excellence that can have the greatest positive impact on your career and your income. Once you know what that is, pour all your energies into becoming the best you can possibly be in that key area." This area of excellence that Tracy and Fraser are referring to is what I call your Strength Zone. The rest of this book will be focused on taking you down the path of discovery to your individual Strength Zone.

Now, besides efficiency in your work and lack of frustration in your role(s), one of the ways that you will be able to tell if you are in your Strength Zone is if you feel energized with your work and with your life. When you can't wait to get back to your work, or to get back to your project because you love it so much, this is a great indication that you are working in your area of strength. In his book *Journey of Desire*, John Eldredge states this eloquently:

There is a secret set within each of our hearts... It is the desire for life as it was meant to be... You may not always be aware of your search, and there are times when you seem to have abandoned looking altogether. But again and again it returns to us, this yearning that cries out for the life we prize...

The greatest human tragedy is to give up the search. Nothing is of greater importance than the life of our deep heart. To lose heart is to lose everything. And if we are to bring our hearts along in our life's journey, we simply must not, we cannot, abandon this desire...

A clue about who we really are and why we are here comes to us through our heart's desire. But it comes in surprising ways, and often it goes unnoticed or is misunderstood. Once in a while, life comes together for us in a way that feels good and right. It feels like what we have been waiting for. These are the moments in our lives that we wish could go on forever. They aren't necessarily the Kodak moments – the weddings and births and great achievements. More often they come in subtle, unexpected ways, as if to sneak up on us.

Think of the times in your life that made you wish that you had the power to make time stand still. Are they not moments of love, moments of joy? Simple moments of rest and quiet when all seems to be well. Something in your heart says, "Finally, it has come. This is what I was made for!"

What I have set out to do in this book is to create a process to help you discover "what you were made for." I do this by showing you how to define your own individual Strength Zone. Your individual Strength Zone has four components:

1. Your values
2. Your personality profile or behavior style
3. Your talents
4. The overlapping area between your values, personality, and talents

The goal of this book is to help you realize your abilities, your areas of excellence. It will help you find what you were made for. It will lead you through the process of defining your values, personality, and talents, and it will show you how they combine into your Strength Zone. It will then be up to you to take this understanding and build yourself into a tower of strength within your Strength Zone.

Summary

1.   To be successful in life, career, and business, you must be more effective and efficient than those around you.

2.   To maximize your effectiveness and efficiency, you must identify your Strength Zone.

3.   An individual's Strength Zones are defined as your values, personality, and talents.

4.   The overlap between your values, personality, and talents is your Overall Strength Zone.

5.   Once your Strength Zone has been defined, you must redefine your approach to each of your roles to fully utilize your Strength Zone.

6.   You must spend time building skills and knowledge in your Strength Zone to become even more effective and efficient.

Activity

1. Do you already know what some of your Strength Zone may be? Try listing them below and then compare back to this as you work through the rest of the book.

2. Before proceeding any further, take some time to identify areas in your personal life and professional life where you know you need to improve because you are not in your Strength Zone. You know this is causing frustration and/or inefficiencies in your work.

3. How much are these inefficiencies costing your employer? How much are they costing you?

4. Do you have others working for you or with you that you suspect are not in their Strength Zone? Are they inefficient or frustrated? How much does this cost your business?

www.StrengthZone.ca

Values

· 2 ·

I believe that it is more of a phenomenon of a wrong value system than it is the age group in which it occurs. All of a sudden you realize that the ladder you've been climbing is leaning against the wrong wall.

~ James Dobson

To remain healthy, your work must be in alignment with your values.

~ John C. Maxwell

Defining your Strength Zone requires first that you understand your values. But what exactly are values? What do you value most? Least? How do your values affect your interactions with people? Are values set, or do they change?

What are values?

Let's start with the Random House *Webster's Dictionary* definition of values:

> *The abstract concept of what is right or worthwhile. To consider with respect to worth or importance.*

This definition, although articulate, seems rather nebulous. Now consider how Arthur Burk of Plumbline Ministries defines values:

> *A value is an abstract concept that is embraced at the expense of personal comfort.*

This definition suggests that to live in harmony with their values, people are willing to sacrifice their personal comfort. If this is true, these people may even be willing to do things that others do not agree with, so they can stay aligned with their values. But does this definition also suggest that differing values between people, organizations, and ethnic groups may actually cause conflict? Is this some great new discovery?

Of course not. As members of the human race, we have recognized for thousands of years that differing values can and do cause conflict. However, if we respect each other properly, differing values don't have to cause conflict. I would like to propose the following definition of values:

A value is an abstract concept **that a person is willing** *to embrace at the expense of personal comfort.*

Most people will sacrifice their personal comfort for their most important values. It happens often, but if we, as a society, are more aware and respectful of others and their values, we can reduce the rate and severity of values-based conflict. So why don't we spend more time trying to understand each other's values? Why don't we try to ensure that our values are aligned with our organization's values? And if alignment is not possible, why don't we at least try to understand why people react the way they do? Why don't we build a plan to deal with these differences?

The rest of this chapter will provide some tools to help you begin evaluating your own values. The following examples show how values affect interactions in everyday life:

- On September 11, 2001, I was sitting in a bid review meeting in Houston, Texas (about 3,500 miles from my home in Calgary, Alberta) when news of the terrorist attacks on the World Trade Center came via a cell phone call from my wife. The people in the meeting reacted with shock and disbelief. Many, driven by their basic, most important values – *security of self* and *family* – left the meeting to return home. Outside our meeting, many other people across North America, driven by *faith and religious* values, spent time praying for the victims and their families. Others were driven by the values of *loyalty* and *commitment to their country*, and many of these people left their homes and relatives and went to New York City to do what they could to help out. Many members of the New York fire and police departments, driven by the value of *courage*, willingly stepped into harm's way at the site of the tragedy.

- I have an occupation that requires extended travel. Although of late, this has been reduced, there was a point where my travel schedule caused me to feel a great deal of stress and guilt. Why? Because one of my most important values is *family*, and due to my travel, I was neglecting my family.

- What about a case where someone values *fun* more than *quality*? This individual may sacrifice quality on a project by leaving work early to attend a sporting event or concert. However, this could potentially jeopardize the project, along with the individual's relationships with co-workers, and potentially his or her job.

- Conversely, consider someone who values *quality* more than *fun*. If this quality person leaves work early without completing a project, he or she will feel nothing but guilt until the situation is resolved (assuming you could get the person to leave work undone in the first place).

- An extreme example of corporate values not being in alignment with a sector of society might be the dissonance between the values of a strip mining company and those of an environmental group (*maximizing profit* versus *protecting the environment*).

Back in early 2001, before the terrorist attacks, I had been working out of town for an extended time. In all, I had been rotating in and out of town for almost twenty-four months. This was hard on my family and extremely hard on my wife, Kelly. During one rotation back home, while driving one of the kids to an event, I began listening to a radio program aired by Dr. James Dobson. Dr. Dobson spoke about ways that men could score points with their wives and thus strengthen their marriages. He gave the example of a man who planned a surprise weekend retreat for his wife so she could get away from her family-related stress for a few days and do whatever she wanted.

I thought this was a great idea and set out to copy it as soon as possible. Before I left for my next out-of-town rotation, I booked a room at a brand new hotel in Calgary for the evening of the day I returned.

I was very excited. I just knew Kelly would love this gesture. The kids and I planned all kinds of surprises, from preparing cards and buying her favorite magazines to writing her special letters. When I returned to Calgary, I drove home and secretly packed her bag, explaining that we had planned a surprise but that she had to wait until we set it up. I picked up the kids and drove to the hotel, where we decorated the room with the cards, magazines, letters, and even a bottle of wine. Then we went back home – where things took an unexpected turn.

Kelly was unhappy. Between questions about where we were going and what to do with the dog, we managed to get halfway to the hotel before she was reduced to tears. Kelly hated surprises. Not knowing what was going on stressed her beyond belief. At this point, the kids were confused, saying things like, "Dad, you said Mom was going to like our surprise." This just added more stress to the situation. I thought I had better come clean, so I explained how Dr. Dobson said it would be good for her to get away for the weekend.

This brought on one of the most unexpected reactions in our marriage to date. For the second time in a few minutes, she broke down in tears. I was shocked! How could this be? I had thought she would be overwhelmed with relief and gratitude for this respite from the kids and all the associated stress. Choking back sobs, however, she asked me a simple question: "Why would you think I want to get away from you and the kids?"

I suddenly realized that she valued her family more than anything. "I've been waiting for you to come home so that we can all be together again," she sobbed. "Now you're trying to take that away from me!"

It was beginning to make sense. I was asking her to compromise one of her primary values. We stopped at the hotel, picked up our "decorations," and went home to spend the weekend together.

Value-laden conflict has nothing to do with lack of talent, lack of knowledge, lack of skill, or even with personality type. It has everything to do with what one person values more than another person and what that person is willing to embrace at the expense of personal comfort.

We all have different concepts of what we are willing to embrace at the expense of personal comfort. This difference in values is one of the things that makes us different from each other. It is also important to note that individuals within a society must have different values in order for that society to function properly. Can you imagine what would have happened after the events of 9/11 if everyone in the U.S. went home to be with family, and not one person went to the site of the tragedy to provide support and assistance? Or if everyone went to the site, and no one went home to be with the children and other family members who needed support and comforting?

We had many examples of conflicting values between team members on the Lilongwe project. While some of these conflicts had to be managed on a long-term basis, others were resolved quickly. In one instance, two of our technical leads on the project were not getting along while stationed in Houston for a prolonged system hardware test. After spending some time with these individuals, it became apparent to me that one technical lead was a hard-charging, high-output worker who valued *quality* while at work and *fun* when the work was over, while the other lead valued *family* more than *quality* or *fun*. The rub came when the hard-charging lead expected everyone to start early in the morning and work late without a lunch break, and then go out partying with the whole team in the evening. The other lead wanted to take a more relaxed lunch hour and then spend the evening in his hotel room talking to his wife on the phone or surfing on the Internet. This lead was willing to take criticism from the other team lead because his personal values were more important to him than his personal comfort. We quickly resolved this potentially volatile situation using some basic team-building exercises.

The power of values is illustrated in the movie *Braveheart*. In the movie, a group of Scots aligned themselves into a formidable force by buying into a common value: freedom. For years, Scottish men, women, and children had been brutalized by the English. This oppression had forced the Scots to live impoverished lives under the constant threat of physical violence.

As the story goes, some English soldiers killed the wife of William Wallace, a Scot. Wallace, driven over the edge, rallied a few men and attacked some English forces, killing them all. This led to a Scottish uprising. Wallace was able to quickly grow his force into a large contingent of untrained, undisciplined, and ill-equipped soldiers.

At a pivotal point in the uprising, the English lined up on one side of a battlefield, and the Scots lined up on the other side. Wallace's force, up against a much larger, well-trained, well-disciplined, and well-equipped English military, was afraid. Instead of fighting, one veteran soldier wanted to run away.

Riding defiantly out in front of his troops, Wallace shouted, "I am William Wallace. And my enemies do not go away... I see a whole army of my countrymen, here in defiance of tyranny. You have come to fight as free men. And free men you are! What will you do with freedom? Will you fight?"

"Two thousand, against ten? We will run – and live!" replied the veteran.

"Yes. Fight and you may die. Run and you will live, at least awhile. And dying in your bed many years from now, would you be willing to trade all the days from this day to that, for one chance to come back here as young men, and tell our enemies that they may take our lives, but they will never take our freedom?"

The Scottish forces, of course, rallied around the common value of *freedom*. They won this battle, and many others. After many battles, however, Wallace was finally captured by the English and executed, suffering a long, brutal, agonizing death. His dying message to the Scottish people was one word: "Freedom!"

That word echoed throughout England and Scotland, inspiring the Scots to victory in other battles. Eventually, they won their freedom, as illustrated by the following extract from the movie:

> In the year of our Lord 1314, patriots of Scotland, starving and outnumbered, charged the fields of Bannockburn. They fought like warrior poets. They fought like Scotsmen. And won their freedom. Forever.

To summarize, I believe that values are best described as *an abstract concept that a person is willing to embrace at the expense of personal comfort.*

Why are values important?

Values drive individual behavior. Your values are like a compass. This compass does not point north, south, east, or west. It points to what is right. Every decision you make is guided by this compass. It is imperative that you clearly understand and can articulate your values. This articulation is similar to a properly calibrated compass. When you understand your values, you will have the confidence to challenge the status quo based on what you believe. You will be able to make decisions confidently and consistently, and you will be able to explain the reasoning behind your decisions.

People who do not have clearly articulated values, or who have no values at all, are like ships without sails being tossed about on stormy seas, drifting wherever life takes them. These people are not consistent in their decision-making, as they have nothing on which to base their decisions. They just go wherever the wind blows. This can have a disastrous effect on them personally and on the people around them.

When the Lilongwe production vessel (FPSO) was being constructed in Korea, it was hit by a typhoon. The FPSO was about three football fields long and about ten stories high. An unpowered vessel, it did not have a rudder. The typhoon blew the FPSO, its moorings, and part of the quayside out to sea. Then the typhoon blew it back toward shore, where it collided with, and crushed, a berthed freighter. Fortunately for our project, the FPSO was only slightly damaged, although the freighter was a write-off.

Unfortunately, this is what happens to individuals who do not have clearly defined values. Without values to securely anchor them, and without engines and a rudder to keep them powered and on track, when the storm hits, they end up causing a lot of damage to themselves and to others.

One of the key ingredients in a successful employee is a stable values base – with *integrity* being one of the most vital. For example, Jed, a newly hired employee, was placed on a design development team in

Calgary. This team worked diligently to deliver a set of fully tested programs to another project team in Korea. The team in Korea was installing the programs and testing them on a system that would then be floated in Russia.

We hired Jed to be a controls systems expert. His resume looked good. He interviewed well, and his limited references seem to check out. His job was to provide quality assurance testing. During the first few weeks, he tested programming and completed the test sheets and signoffs as required. Then we had an urgent need for additional resources in our Korean office. Jed volunteered to go, and we were happy to send him, as he seemed to be moving through his testing work rather quickly.

When Jed arrived in Korea, he began some on-site program testing. This work was similar to what he did back home. He seemed to be doing well. However, a crack in the wall began to appear. We started to get reports about Jed having disagreements with the client in Korea. Then there were reports of people finding errors in the programs Jed had tested and signed off on in Calgary. These reports led to a complete reassessment of the work done in Calgary. It was determined that Jed had just been signing off test sheets without actually doing the testing. We did more investigating and discovered the same thing was happening in Korea, where Jed was again signing off test sheets without doing the appropriate testing. Jed was subsequently brought back to Calgary and terminated for lack of integrity.

According to Paul Zane Pilzer in his book *Unlimited Wealth*, "...a new problem is emerging in the raising of preschool children, to which the problem of rearing more productive children pales by comparison. This problem is one of values – and it is threatening more than just the success of our public educational system; it is threatening the very fabric of our society. Simply stated, far too many of our children are being raised without a sense of the basic, common values that have enabled people to function together and survive as a society."

I have seen several dramatic flameouts with newly hired employees, where the flameout was simply due to a lack of basic values, such as honesty and integrity. I have tried to coach these individuals through this minefield, but what I have found is that skills are much easier to teach than values. If values are not instilled in people at a young age, they can be difficult to teach later in life. Lack of character can be a cancer in an organization; when it is found, action needs to be taken immediately. In every instance where an individual was identified as lacking character, even after extensive coaching, I was forced to remove the person from our company.

Amazing to me in each case was the rest of the team's response after the removal of these individuals. Many of the team members would come to my office and personally thank me for taking action. Even though these people were technically competent, the lack of character was extremely disruptive to the entire team, to the point that some of our high-potential people were thinking about leaving if the disruptive person was not dealt with.

In his book, *Management Challenges for the 21st Century*, Peter Drucker relates the following story about what he experienced with a values conflict in the workplace.

> *But there is sometimes a conflict between a person's values and the same person's strengths. What one does well – even very well – and successfully may not fit with one's value system... If I may interject a personal note: I too, many years ago, had to decide between what I was doing well and successfully, and my values. I was doing extremely well as a young investment banker in London in the mid-1930s; it clearly fitted my strengths. Yet I did not see myself making a contribution as an asset manager of any kind. People, I realized, were my values. And I saw no point in being the richest man in the cemetery. I had no money, no job in a deep Depression, and no prospects. But I quit – and it was the right thing.*

In this story, Drucker walked away from a job because it was making him compromise his values. Drucker felt that it was better to walk away from his position and retain his values than it would be to stay in that position, make lots of money, and have to live each day violating his values.

For you to maximize your performance – either individually, or as a leader, or as part of a team – you have to identify your values and understand how they affect you. You must ensure that you align your actions with your values, because you have to walk your talk. Failure to do this is a violation of your values and will be seen by others as hypocrisy.

This results in lack of credibility and in a loss of positive influence on others.

In the book *Christian Reflections on Leadership Challenge*, James Kouzes and Barry Posner state, "Exemplary leaders find their voice by clarifying their personal values and then expressing those values in their own style. They then set the example by aligning their personal actions with shared values." According to Kouzes and Posner, the first step in becoming a leader is to "find your voice." That means defining or articulating your values. The second step is to set the example by aligning your actions with these values. Don't just talk about your values. Walk your talk.

What happens, if for some reason, you violate your values? Take, for example, a businessman who violates one or more of his values to make a sale or just to get ahead. Violation of values can cause depression, guilt, anger, and resentment (just to name a few of the side effects). Victory can taste bitter if you violate your fundamental values to win. The side effects can be even worse if others witness your actions. Regardless of how well you cover your tracks, someone will always know what has happened – even if that person is you. This reminds me of a verse my parents taught me: "Be sure that your sins will find you out."

A victory that can be credited, in part or in whole, to some violation of values will destroy your credibility and your positive influence over others. Most great scandals in recent times can be tracked to the violation of fundamental values. Take, for example, former U.S. presidents Nixon and Clinton, Jimmy Baker, Jimmy Swaggart, Enron, and WorldCom. In each of these cases, the fundamental values of people, organizations, corporations or countries were violated. This violation resulted, among other things, in the loss of credibility of the leaders involved, and in many cases, it destroyed the lives of those leaders.

Keep in mind, however, that should you make a mistake and violate a value, it does not mean that you are forever doomed. What it does mean is that you must spend time reestablishing your values and aligning your actions with those values. You may never again attain the level of influence that you enjoyed before the violation occurred, or you might possibly attain a higher level of positive influence. It depends on how hard you work at it.

Chuck Colson is an excellent example of this. Implicated and indicted in the Watergate scandal, he ended up serving time in jail. There, he realized he had not violated just one of his values; in the quest for power, he had, over time, sold out his values completely. Winifred Gallagher describes Colson as follows: "Charles Colson would have beat his grandmother to death when he was with Nixon. However, the Watergate event changed him completely, and since his release from prison, he has positively influenced more people than he ever would have as part of the Nixon administration... He probably always had a very emotional, intense temperament, but now he has different enemies and friends. His nature didn't change – he just does something else with all that zeal. One's mode of engagement with life may not alter much. But one's focus can."

How do values affect you as you strive for victory? What can you do to ensure that your values remain intact while you struggle to succeed in your endeavors? Is it even possible to attain victory while keeping your values intact?

In most cases, it *is* possible to maintain your values and still win. If you have to violate your values to succeed, it is better to lose. Losing while retaining your values and integrity is better than violating your values to "win." This relates back to the definition of value: "*A value is an abstract concept that a person is willing to embrace at the expense of personal comfort.*" If you are not willing to maintain a value at the expense of personal comfort, maybe the value in question is not one of yours.

Values are important because they drive and guide you as an individual. Every decision you make, every action you take, is driven by your values. Without values, you will wander aimlessly throughout life. Violating your values can destroy you as a person, and it can destroy the lives of others around you.

Perfect value combination

There is no such thing as a perfect set of values. Every person has the ability and the freedom to chose and live his or her own values. Most people already realize this, but the thing that many people miss is that they do not have the right to impose their values onto other people. This has been a source of conflict for thousands of years. People must voluntarily select their values and then respect the values of others in their personal and professional lives.

People's values are formed throughout life, and often those values mature and change as they get older. Many factors come into play. Formation of values can be influenced by:

- Parents
- Siblings
- Extended family members
- Friends
- Enemies
- Teachers
- Personalities
- Talents
- Religious upbringing
- Church environment
- School environment
- Political environment
- Physical environment
- Education
- Health
- Employer
- Career
- Social status
- Sports teams
- Financial status
- Marital status
- Family status
- Uplifting events
- Traumatic events
- Achievements or lack of achievements

As you can see from this list, people form their values through a complicated network of interwoven influences. The biggest influences tend to be parents, friends, religion, personality, and talents, although not necessarily in that order. Two people who grow up in the same household with basically the same influences can grow up with entirely different values. Most siblings have one or two values in common, but their other values can be significantly different.

With the formation of values based on so many different influences, the potential combination of values is staggering (this is the mathematician coming out in me). It is easy to see why most people have differing values, and it is easy to see why there are no perfect value combinations. Everyone is unique. We see and respond to our environment in unique ways. This unique perception is what causes us to have our own set of values.

What do you value?

So what do you value? Have you ever stopped to figure this out?

To help you answer this all-important question, I've provided a list of values below. The best way to approach this exercise is to read the list of values and associated definitions while asking yourself, "What would I be willing to embrace at the expense of personal comfort?" In other words, "What am I willing to stand up for?" It can help to ask yourself questions such as:

- What deeply motivates me to action?

- What things cause me to be de-motivated and to withdraw?

- What started, and then fueled, the major arguments I have had at home, work, church, in restaurants or stores, or even at parties?

- What makes me feel cornered or threatened?

Think of a major event that took place in your life. What did this event inspire you to do? What did it make you think of? If you were not inspired by that event, why not? What kept you from being inspired? Think of a major world event that has taken place in your lifetime – maybe it was the assassination of John Fitzgerald Kennedy, or the Oklahoma City bombing, 9/11, the fall of the Iron Curtain, or the demolition of the Berlin Wall. What did this event inspire you to do? What did it make you think of? If you were not inspired, why not? What was going on in your life that kept you from being inspired?

It all comes down to this: "What makes you step out of your comfort zone and sacrifice your personal comfort?"

As you go through this exercise, keep in mind that my list of values is not exhaustive. I'm sure that many other values are not listed. The idea of putting this list together came to me following two events. First, I finished working through a conflict resolution series published by the Center for Creative Leadership (www.centerforcreativeleadership.com). CCL asserted that one of the biggest reasons for conflict in the workplace was conflicting values. It advocated sorting out the values held by both parties to see if this could be a source of the conflict.

Second, I attended a John C. Maxwell seminar where "value" cards were provided. Maxwell gave course attendees just a few minutes to sort through their cards and pick their top six values (www.maximumimpact.com). He went through this exercise to show how important values are to those in leadership positions and how their values may cause conflict with the people they are leading. I found this exercise to be a real eye-opener for many people.

If you think you may have one or more values that are not on this list, by all means add them. Just jot them down underneath the list or in the margin. The other thing to keep in mind is that the definitions I've provided may not be exactly what you think. That's okay. These definitions work for me, but they are not perfect. If you think of something else when you read a value, just replace my definition with yours. The outcome of this exercise is to help you determine your most important values, not to quibble over definitions.

The process of determining values should be revisited periodically. I tend to take a detailed look at what I value once a year, but some people may also want to review their values during times of stress. In times of great stress, what a person really values becomes very apparent.

When you come to the list below, stop. Review the list, sorting through the values for yourself, and pick your top six values. Let me repeat that advice: take the time to review these values. Sort them into categories according to High, Medium, and Low importance. When you have completed this, select the six most important values from the high-importance category and write them below.

 Note that the following list is available for download at www.StrengthZone.ca.

Values	Definition
Accountable	Take responsibility for outcome/actions
Achievement	Strive for the completion of your goals. Once one is done you must start on the next.
Action or Urgency	Need for immediate action and quick results
Affluence	High income or prosperity
Analytical	The ability to apply logic and analyze many different solutions/possibilities when addressing problems/issues
Authority or Power	Having the opportunity to control events and activities of others
Balance	Giving the proper time and priority to all areas of your life
Challenge	Gets energy from accepting and meeting challenges
Change	Valuing change and continuous improvement
Commitment	Take ownership for anything that you commit to
Community	Working towards and supporting goals or a purpose that may not always align with personal desires
Competence	Being able to effectively perform in an area or areas
Competition	The need to perform at a top level in everything
Confidence	A firm belief in yourself and abilities
Consistent	The need or perform or behave in a consistent manner
Courage	Strength to stand up for what you believe in
Creativity/Innovation	Using your imagination and innovation to discover or develop new ideas or things
Customer Satisfaction	Striving to ensure that customers receive the highest level of service
Diversity or Tolerance	Ability to respect diverse people/cultures/lifestyles

Values	Definition
Diplomacy	Having tact when dealing with others
Economic Security	Secure employment where financial needs are met
Effectiveness	Producing the desired effect to achieve results
Efficiency	Producing the desired effect in a timely manner without waste
Fairness	The desire to treat everyone equally
Faith/Religion	Belief in a supernatural power
Family	Spending time with your family (immediate and/or extended)
Fitness	To stay in shape physically, mentally, and emotionally
Friendship	Being with friends or building new friendships
Fun	Humorous, able to laugh, lightheartedness
Growth	The desire to continually learn and develop yourself
Happiness	A state of well being and contentment
Harmony	The need to avoid conflict
Helping Others	Always ready and willing to go out of your way to help others
Honesty	To be truthful
Humor	Good spirits, always positive and cheerful
Independence or Freedom	Freedom from influence or control of others
Inspiration	Needing to inspire self and/or others
Integrity	Trustworthiness. Adherence to a strict code of values, moral, or ethical standards both when people are looking and when they are not.
Interactive	The need to work with others and not independently
Knowledge	Program of or pursuit of continual learning and understanding
Legacy	Making a difference that will impact future generations
Love	To be involved in affectionate, intimate relationships

Values	Definition
Loyalty	Dedication and faithfulness
Passion	Strong emotional feeling; intense enthusiasm.
Patience	The ability to deal with things during times of stress and annoyance or to deal with things over a period of time
Perfection	Striving for perfection in everything that is done
Persuasion	The need to win people over to a way of thinking, idea, plan or concept
Popularity	The need to be in a good social standing in every social setting
Positive	Always having a positive outlook on circumstances
Quality	Striving for a defined standard of excellence
Recognition	The need for receiving and giving recognition for work performed
Reflection	Thinking back on past events and applying them to current situations
Risk	The need for activities with a higher level of risk
Self-Respect	High level of self-confidence, self-worth, and self-esteem
Simplicity	Freedom from complexity
Status	Position of prestige
Stability	To avoid upheaval and change; status quo
Structure	The need for and complying with processes and systems
Teamwork	Having cooperative relationships with a group of people in a working environment
Trust	To rely on another's integrity or character
Volunteerism/Service	Providing a service above what is required typically for no remuneration
Wisdom	The ability to compare knowledge, understanding, and experience and determine the proper course of action

Activity

Note: If you want to get maximum value from this book, it is essential that you take the time to do this exercise. This activity is also available online at www.StrengthZone.ca

Pick your top six values:

1)

2)

3)

4)

5)

6)

Now pick your top two values:

1)

2)

There is no correct combination of values. Everyone is unique. You will value something more (or less) than the next person. However, the two values that you just selected are vital to your emotional, mental, and even physical well-being. Never, for any reason, violate these values.

1.   What have you learned about yourself from this exercise?

2.   Can you see how your values may conflict with someone else's values under certain circumstances (*quality* versus *quantity*)?

3.   Can you see how your values would work well with someone else's values?

4.   Are there situations in your life where you need to re-evaluate decisions or actions and realign them with your values?

My top two values are *faith* and *family*, followed by *integrity*, *wisdom*, *achievement*, and *courage*. Some of my co-workers have the same top two values as me, but most are quite different.

Differences in values have the potential to cause conflict in the workplace. Some examples of the conflicts I have seen include:

- *Family* versus *career.* Earlier in this chapter, I described how my extensive work-related travel caused stress for my family and me. Other examples include choosing between important meetings at work and my children's performances at school, or between work and parent-teacher interviews.

- *Quality* versus *quantity.* We had situations on the Lilongwe project where team members had to deliver a lot of programming work in a short period of time. Some team members could really pump out code, and progress looked great until a quality check showed the acceptable error rate was too high. *Quantity* has to balance with *quality.* On the flipside, some engineers spent far too much time perfecting their work. This cost the project money and caused frustration with other team members.

- *Integrity* versus *affluence.* Examples of this conflict on the Lilongwe project included overcharging for hours or, more clearly, individuals charging for hours that were not necessarily productive in an attempt to maximize their pay.

- *Creativity* versus *quantity.* In a fast-track project, the tendency is always to do things the way they have always been done and to avoid creativity because it adds risk. On the Lilongwe project, we were building a configuration tool we thought would save us time and money, but the tool was undeveloped, and there was no precedent because it had never been done. In fact, we did not know if it would work until the day we had to use it. This caused a lot of stress. Some members of the team wanted to go back to the old way of coding – although the old way was much slower, it was well-defined and reliable. Fortunately, the tool worked, and in the end, it saved us a lot of money.

- *Perfection* versus *quantity.* This is similar to *quality* versus *quantity*, except that the perfectionists on Lilongwe could not bear the thought of sending out "Volkswaggoned" work. They wanted to spend way too much time adding "Cadillac" features and functionality. These features would have been nice to have, but they were not required, and they may not even have been recognized or appreciated by the client.

- ***Reflection*** versus ***urgency.*** People who value *reflection* like to spend time thinking about past projects, trying to apply the knowledge they gained in the past to their present projects. On a fast-track project, however, it can be difficult to find time to reflect on anything, as everyone is struggling to meet the urgent schedules.

- ***Independence*** versus ***structure.*** One of our technical leads was extremely independent. He believed that he brought more to our company than anyone else and that the processes and systems he had been taught at his previous company were much superior to those at our company. He was unwilling to change his approach, to adapt to our way of doing business. As a result, he was removed from his lead role until he was willing to work as part of the team.

When you do run into conflict, in or outside the workplace, it may not be due to values, but this is usually the first area that should be examined. There have been many conflict resolution processes published over the years, so I will not go into any detail here, other than to describe a high-level resolution process as it relates to values.

Obviously, the first thing that needs to be done is to define the problem. This is done by gathering the information related to the conflict – being careful to consider all options and each perspective. This must be done in a non-partisan fashion with an open mind to both sides of the conflict. If you are not able to examine the issue without bias, you may have to remove yourself from the process and bring in a third party. Part of the information gathering should include a detailed look at the values of the individuals from each side of the conflict. This can be done by taking the values list presented earlier in this chapter and having each individual sort this list into three categories: Important, Sometimes Important, and Rarely Important.

Once this sorting has been completed, the results for each individual involved should be compared. The differences in values can be very obvious, but they can also be vague, so they must be examined in detail. It can be very valuable to have each side of the conflict to work through an exercise where they switch roles and switch values, "walk a mile in the others shoes", so to speak. This will help each individual understand the other's point of view and will accentuate the need for everyone to work positively with each other.

What are corporate values?

Corporate values can be defined in much the same way as we defined individual values.

A corporate value is an abstract concept that a corporation is willing to embrace at the expense of corporate comfort.

Typically, corporate values are set by leaders whose behavior exemplifies their personal beliefs and who have convinced the organization that these values would be of benefit to everyone. This is not necessarily an easy transition. A leader cannot just show up and arbitrarily impose his or her values on a company, summarily expecting everyone to buy into these beliefs. This has been tried in many organizations, and it typically leads to rebellion, or worse, forced compliance, instead of voluntary buy-in.

An effective leader must define corporate values in cooperation with the organization. This leader must honor diversity but stress common values. Stressing common values does not mean that the leader must whitewash or dilute his or her vision for the organization's values. It simply means that the leader must understand the organization and determine the values that can be shared while still meeting the vision or purpose of the organization. These shared values must not violate individual values, and the shared values must actually be shared. They cannot just be the leader's idea of shared values. The process must be a joint effort between the leader and the organization. The values must be established by agreement. These shared values will form the basis for productive relationships within the organization. If the organization has bought into these values, individuals within the organization will align themselves with the values, this creates a common purpose for all individuals and allows the organization to build positive momentum.

Once these shared values are defined, the leader must make sure that they are modeled in every aspect of the organization, from the boardroom to everyday operations. The leader must align his or her actions with the shared values. In doing this, the leader sets an example that everyone in the organization will follow. The leader is building a positive influence with the organization. The actions that a leader takes in modeling shared corporate values can make the difference between an extraordinarily successful organization and an organization that is doomed to mediocrity.

Ralph Waldo Emerson stated this eloquently when he wrote, "Your actions speak so loudly I cannot hear what you say." A leader needs to ensure that his or her actions align with the spoken messages. People can, and will, see through any façade. For example, when employees criticize GreedyCompany.com for not stating its values, it quickly launches an internal campaign defining those values. The campaign is intended to get employees to align their personal goals with those of the organization. However, the employees know that the values defined in the internal campaign are eclipsed by the company's actions, which are clearly aligned around only one thing – operating profit. This misalignment causes frustration on all fronts – with employees and with management.

Like personal values, corporate values drive the behavior of the corporation. Having shared values within the organization results in:

- Less stress on individuals
- Less tension between individuals and departments
- Enthusiasm in the workplace
- Pride in work
- Direction in the workplace
- Less bureaucracy
- Positive attitudes
- Positive momentum

Corporate values should be limited in number to three or four. More than that is too many. People will have a hard time focusing on what is most important. Similarly, corporate values must be ranked from most important to least important. Without this ranking, everyone in the corporation will assign their own priorities to the core values. This could cause some surprising and unexpected results. For example, Disney's values are defined in order of priority as *safety, courtesy, show*, and *efficiency*. This allows employees to pre-empt efficiency of operations with safety issues, courtesy to customers, and showmanship. It means that employees dealing with customers in a courteous manner can leave these customers should a safety issue arise. If these values were defined in a different order, Disney employees could sacrifice personal safety to improve the show or to enhance efficiency. Obviously, this is an extreme example and would not happen, but it does illustrate the need to assign priorities to values.

A great example of an organization that requires its members to be totally aligned with its values is the U.S. Army. Its values are:

Loyalty – bear true faith and allegiance to the U.S. constitution, the army, your unit, and other soldiers.

Duty – fulfill your obligations.

Respect – treat people as they should be treated.

Selfless service – put the welfare of the nation, the army, and your subordinates before your own.

Honor – live up to all the army values.

Integrity – do what's right, legally and morally.

Personal courage – face fear, danger, or adversity (physical or moral).

The values of the U.S. Navy are similar:

Honor. "I will bear true faith and allegiance..." Accordingly, we will: conduct ourselves in the highest ethical manner in all relationships with peers, superiors, and subordinates; be honest and truthful in our dealings with each other and with those outside the navy; be willing to make honest recommendations and accept those of junior personnel; encourage new ideas and deliver the bad news, even when it is unpopular; abide by an uncompromising code of integrity, taking responsibility for our actions and keeping our word; fulfill or exceed our legal and ethical responsibilities in our public and personal lives twenty-four hours a day. Illegal or improper behavior or even the appearance of such behavior will not be tolerated. We are accountable for our professional and personal behavior. We will be mindful of the privilege to serve our fellow Americans.

Courage. "I will support and defend..." Accordingly, we will have: courage to meet the demands of our profession and the mission when it is hazardous, demanding, or otherwise difficult; make decisions in the best interest of the navy and the nation, without regard to personal consequences; meet these challenges while adhering to a higher standard of personal conduct and decency; be loyal to our nation, ensuring the resources entrusted to us are used in an honest, careful, and efficient way. Courage is the value that gives us the moral and mental strength to do what is right, even in the face of personal or professional adversity.

Commitment. "I will obey the orders..." Accordingly, we will: demand respect up and down the chain of command; care for the safety, professional, personal and spiritual well-being of our people; show respect toward all people without regard to race, religion, or gender; treat each individual with human dignity; be committed to positive change and constant improvement; exhibit the highest degree of moral character, technical excellence, quality, and competence in what we have been trained to do. The day-to-day duty of every navy man and woman is to work together as a team to improve the quality of our work, our people, and ourselves.

The most feared military organizations in the world didn't achieve their level of effectiveness by simply handing weapons to a bunch of 18-year-old boys and wishing them good luck. They are what they are today because they aligned themselves with their core values. They take untrained and undisciplined boys out of high school and turn them into the world's most disciplined and effective fighting machine. This training and discipline is focused around core values – values, which must not, under any circumstances, be violated.

I realize that this is an extreme example of alignment around core values, but corporations like Wal-Mart, Disney, and Home Depot have done a similar thing in the corporate world. They have turned their corporations into dominant entities within their markets by aligning their employees around consistent corporate values.

In my experience, when management fails to define, align with, and model corporate values, employees typically exhibit the following behaviors:

1. Individuals attempting to align with what they personally value most highly.

2. Individuals attempting to align with what they think the company values.

3. Individuals becoming discouraged, unfocused, unproductive, bitter, and resentful.

Project values

Corporate values can, and should, be used on a project level. Up front, I established project-specific values on the Lilongwe project. My intent was not to tell the team that these were project values, as at the time, I had not yet fully grasped the power of shared values. My intent was to establish some ground rules for the execution of the project, so that there could be no misconceptions among team members.

Everyone new to the project received the following email from me:

To:

Subject: **Welcome to the Lilongwe project!**

The Lilongwe project is a first, in many regards, for us. Some of these are listed below:

It is the first project that we have received as a Main Instrumentation and Controls Contractor (MICC).

It is the first major project with <Our Client> where a MICC's services have been employed.

It is the first major DeltaV project for both us and <Our Client>.

It is the first major safety integrated system project for us.

It is the first major offshore facility project for us.

It is the first project where object linking and embedding for process control has played such an important role towards the overall project success.

It is the first project where a process simulator has been a major part of the project.

Having pointed out all these firsts, it is important to note that our individual team members have had a lot of experience in all of these areas in the past (other than the obvious item #1). However, we are bringing a lot of "firsts" together, and because of this, we need to pull together as a cohesive team in order to make this project the resounding success that I know it can be. Our success on this project to date (during the front end engineering and design portion: FEED) has resulted in us being considered for many other major projects with <Our Client> so we want to make a good showing on the post FEED portion and continue to give <Our Client> the high level of service that they have come to expect from us.

The Lilongwe project is distributed between Houston (location of <Our Client>), Holland (construction location of engineering contractor #1), Korea (construction location of engineering contractor #2), Calgary (us), and Angola (final location of the facility).

The project director for this project is handled by Fred in Houston. Fred is assisted in Houston by John (interface manager to engineering contractor #1), Jack (interface manager to engineering contractor #2) and a yet to be assigned individual. The operations in Calgary are being managed by me, Dave Taylor.

As can be seen from the number of players in this project and the geographical distribution of design and construction teams, the logistics involved in completing this project successfully are quite complicated. Efficient communication between all parties is essential.

It is also important to note that this is a fixed price or lump sum project. This means that we estimated the amount of work required to complete this project and finalized a price between us and <Our Client>. This price can only be modified if the input/output count changes or if the scope of the project changes. The modifications themselves are also governed by a contract (i.e., an additional analog output costs x$ and an analog input costs n$).

What I am getting at…this means that Fred and I will be tracking the project closely to ensure that every hour charged results in a productive hour worked. We cannot tolerate unproductive hours as this comes straight out of the profit margin for the project.

Although we have many challenges ahead of us on this project, I know that it will be completed successfully if we all work together as a team. Please feel free to call, drop me an email, or stop by my office (but not all three), if you have any project related questions or concerns.

Thanks

Dave Taylor, P.Eng.

From this email, you can see that I outlined the following values, although they were not specifically stated as values:

- Quality
- Quantity
- Productivity
- Efficiency
- Integrity
- Teamwork
- Competence

Much of our success on Lilongwe can be attributed to the fact that the project team members were, for the most part, aligned in their professional values based on the simple outline in this email. These values were not just stated once in the email and forgotten, they were continually stated and restated. We did this in our daily interactions, in our weekly review meetings, and in the reports that we distributed weekly to all project team members. These values were modeled by me and by all the technical team leaders.

Deviations from these values were dealt with when they occurred. Most people did not have issues with these values, but for the few that did, most deviated no more than once. However, a small number of individuals were removed from the project due to repeated issues over values, and at least one person was removed from the project (and the company) due to integrity issues. I always told the team leaders that I would rather have a person of integrity and questionable intelligence than a person of great intelligence but questionable integrity. On Lilongwe, I needed people I could trust. If they did not have skills in certain areas, they had to be intelligent enough to know it and honest enough to tell me, so that we could find this skill before it was too late and mistakes were made. Fortunately, on the Lilongwe project, I had team leaders with both intelligence and integrity.

As successful as we were, however, I believe that we could have been even more effective had I presented my initial email with more clarity, and especially, if I had defined the values instead of burying them inconspicuously within the body of the message. I have used similar emails (but more clearly articulated) for projects since Lilongwe, and I plan to use similar messages on all future projects.

The best leader of all time lived two thousand years ago. In the first sermon Jesus ever recorded, he defined a list of core values required for his followers (Matthew 6:1 – 7:27). He summarized these values in Matthew 7:12 with a single statement: "Therefore whatever you want men to do to you, do also to them." This is known as the Golden Rule.

All great leaders understand the requirement for harmony and productivity. The way to achieve this is to ensure that all people within the organization focus on common values.

Are personal values different than corporate values?

Personal values can be different than corporate values. In most cases, they should be different.

Corporate values are established to serve the corporation, its employees, and its customers. These values must align with personal values, but they don't have to be the same. Take the Disney example again. Disney's values are *safety, courtesy, show,* and *efficiency.* Most family-oriented people would not choose *efficiency* over spending time with family. However, working at Disney does not force a family-oriented person to violate the value of *family.* It simply means that the person's values must be aligned with Disney's values while at work. They are sharing values.

Disney understands that an employee may have to leave work should a family member become injured or sick. The company would never force that employee to remain working so it could operate a show more efficiently. Disney understands that would violate all their values (*safety*, *courtesy*, *show*, and *efficiency* would all be negatively affected due to the employee's concern about the family member). This is what shared values are all about.

In cases where corporate values do violate or negatively impact personal values, action must be taken. The corporation must decide if it needs to realign its values to better serve its employees. If the organization does not choose realignment, the individual must decide if he or she can continue working in that environment. Typically, the individual will have to move into a different line of work. Failure to move out of that environment will only result in continued stress and job dissatisfaction.

As extreme examples, consider an animal rights activist working at a meat packing plant or an environmentalist working in a strip-mining operation. These people would continually run into values-based issues – meatpacking plants cannot stay in operation if they don't pack meat, while strip-mining companies have to dig up the earth to find and refine their product. I'm sure there are situations where an animal rights activist could make the meat processing procedure more humane, but you can only go so far. The same goes for the strip-mining company.

If the Lilongwe values were defined as quality, quantity, productivity, efficiency, integrity, teamwork, and competence, we can see a potential conflict between a team member, whose top personal value is *family*. The project leader may expect this person to deliver a lot of work (*quantity*) with a low error rate (*quality*) in a very short time (*efficiency*). However, the project values would all be violated if this person had a family issue but was "forced" to remain at work to achieve the quantity, quality, and efficiency that the project expected. The person would be consumed with the neglected family issue, and as a result, the quality, quantity, and efficiency of his or her work would be compromised. Obviously, it would be much better to allow the person to take care of the family issue, then return to work able to properly concentrate. Note, however, that there is a balance here. People who continually have problems that take them away from work perhaps need to move on to another company, one that allows them to spend more time away from work without negatively impacting their output.

Should these people change their values so they can retain their jobs? Probably not. If the values they are expressing are real and fundamental, they need to remove themselves from the situation or they will always be in turmoil.

Can you (or should you) change your values?

Your values, like an organization's values, can change over time. However, this change must not be made just to fit in or to try to make a sale. That would not be a change in values. It would be a violation of values – and as previously discussed, violation of values only results in personal turmoil, stress, and loss of credibility.

However, values will change over time. In fact, they should change as an individual grows and matures. When I was growing up, for example, one of my most important values was *fun*. I loved playing sports, fishing, hunting, riding my dirt bike, and many other activities. As I grew older and more mature (the mature part is still debatable), my most important values shifted. In particular, the *fun* value was replaced by my *family* value.

I think the turning point came on February 16, 1989. It was my wife's birthday. I was in the fourth year of my engineering degree. Kelly and I had gotten married over summer break, and this was her first birthday as a married woman.

I have always loved hockey. I started playing while quite young and played each season, including throughout my university years. Although I never considered the sport anything but fun and exercise, I have a competitive spirit, and as luck would have it, my team was good enough to make the playoffs in 1989. One of our most important games happened to fall on February 16. I was smart enough to ask my new bride if it would be all right if, after we went out for her birthday dinner, I could drop her at home and go to the arena. I was not smart enough to realize that when she said yes she really meant no.

As we progressed through dinner, she grew increasingly quiet. When it came time for me to drop her at home, she asked a profoundly simple, but very confusing, question: "Are you really going to your game?"

"Of course," I replied, somewhat taken aback. "I'm going to the game because you said it was okay with you."

We arrived at home, and I proceeded to round up my equipment and get ready to leave. She continued to ask subtle questions, but being newly married and smart as a sack of hammers about women, I just cheerfully answered her questions and headed out the door, pumped for the big game.

About halfway to the university, I realized that I had forgotten my ID card. Without it, I could not play. I headed back home in a panic, trying to figure out how I could get the card and not be late for the game. When I arrived home, I found my wife in tears. I finally clued in. Even though she had said yes, she really wanted me to spend the evening with her on her birthday. Consequently, I did not leave for the arena and missed the game.

That evening, I realized some things were more important than having fun. My values changed. Although my career has required me to travel extensively, since the first year of our marriage, I have never missed being at home for my wife's birthday.

So a person's values should change over time, based on the maturing process and the progression through life. The only caveat is that this change in values must not be a short-term, temporary change made to justify a less-than-honest business or personal decision. The change must be well thought out and based on deep-seated personal beliefs. You cannot change your values to fit the moment.

Conclusion

Identifying your values is the first step in defining your Strength Zone. In fact, this can be called your Values Strength Zone. Understanding your values is the cornerstone of understanding and working in your Overall Strength Zone. Working within your values can be an energizing experience. Working outside your values, or in violation of your values, can be devastating. By helping others around you define their values, and work within their values, you build on their strengths. This helps build the strength and cohesion of your team. As James Dobson says, you want to ensure that the ladder you are climbing is leaning against the correct wall.

Summary

1.   Values are "an abstract concept that a person is willing to embrace at the expense of personal comfort."

2.   Values are like a compass – they form the basis for every decision that you make in life.

3.   What are your most important values? Identify them and always be aware of them.

4.   Corporate values are "an abstract concept that corporations are willing to embrace at the expense of corporate comfort."

5.   Leaders must always model corporate values.

6.   Personal and corporate values should be shared, but they can be different. The values of the corporation should never violate the values of the individual.

7.   A person's values can change over time, but this change must **not** be made to fit the moment.

 Application exercise

1.   Take the time to do the values definition activity on pages 49 to 54. List your top six values in the order of priority in the chart below. This is your Values Strength Zone.

	Your Values	Spouse/Friend	Corporate
1			
2			
3			
4			
5			
6			

2. Have your spouse, a close friend, or co-worker do this exercise. List their values in the table above.

3. Compare your values with theirs.

- Is there a correlation?

- What are the differences?

- Can you tell which correlating values have helped build the relationship?

- Conversely, which conflicting values have caused friction?

4. Compare your values to your corporate values.

- Does your corporation have clearly defined values?

- Are these values being modeled?

- Can your values be aligned with the corporation's values, or are there irreconcilable differences?

www.StrengthZone.ca

Your Personality Profile

· 3 ·

The most useful person in the world today is the man or woman who knows how to get along with other people. Human relations is the most important science in living.

- Stanley C. Allyn

Fred's, however, don't use people as a means to an end; they use relationships to build a foundation for success. They understand that all outcomes are created by and through interactions with others. So they become students of social psychology. They understand that strong relationships create loyalty and are the basis of partnerships and teamwork.

- The Fred Factor by Mark Sandborn

The ability to deal with people is as purchasable a commodity as sugar or coffee. And I will pay more for that ability than for any other under the sun.

- John D. Rockefeller

Understanding people's values is important, but understanding how different personalities react and interact is probably even more important. The next step in defining your Strength Zone is to learn how to understand your own personality type, how to identify the personalities of co-workers, and how to adapt your interactions to communicate more efficiently with those around you.

What are personalities?

We all know that every person has a unique personality. But how are personalities formed?

It is generally accepted that two factors influence personality: genetics and environment. The study of personality is called behavioral genetics and is conducted by psychologists and geneticists. Dr. Paul Grobstein, a biologist from Bryn Mawr College in Pennsylvania, wrote the following:

The more we understand about genetics, the clearer it becomes that while genetic information significantly influences both development and behavior, it fully determines neither. There is no war between nature (the genome) and nurture (the environment), except in some people's minds. In human development and behavior, as in the development and behavior of all other living organisms, the genome and the environment instead productively interact with one another, both contributing unique and valuable information to the emergence of distinctive individuals. In fact, the more we understand about development and behavior, the more obvious it becomes that nature and nurture are similarly influences rather than determinants, not only singly but also in combination. There is in each of us, and probably in all organisms, an unpredictability in both development and behavior which remains even when all of the information provided by both the genome and by the environment (including culture) is accounted for. Within this relatively unexplored space, there is plenty of room to find a third influence on development and behavior: a "self" which is also real, important, and able, in limited ways, to influence its own fate. As most people also know intuitively, biology cannot subtract from what it is to be human. It can only add to our understanding of all that being human encompasses, and, in so doing, enhance our ability to explore and realize the potentials inherent in humanity itself.

This essentially states that a portion of a child's personality is genetically determined when the child is born. The balance is determined in the first five to ten years of the child's life by the environment in which the child is raised and the third influence "self." Although, I won't go into an indepth discussion on "self," this refers to the ability we have to think and make choices that are outside the biological and environmental influence. A number of studies have validated the genetic/environment personality theory. Some of these studies, involving identical twins separated at birth, found that the twins developed remarkably similar personalities, even though they did not know each other, and the environments in which they grew up were substantially different.

For those of you who have several children, the theory that part of a child's personality is genetic is probably no surprise. Most parents recognize that from birth onward, their children are unique in their behavior. My middle child, Lindsey, was extremely colicky and stubborn. She demonstrated this personality trait by insisting on having things exactly as she wanted them, even at a young age. For example, she would cry if she wasn't held in a particular way or if she was laid down facing the wrong direction. I am not talking about whimpering, either. I'm talking about blood-curdling, earsplitting screams that continued until the situation was fixed.

Lindsey has not outgrown this personality trait. Fortunately, however, she has learned to apply it constructively in many areas of her life. As a result, she is an incredibly good student. She stubbornly refuses to give up, fighting through adversity until she understands and masters new concepts.

My oldest daughter, Brittany, has been easygoing from the time she was born. As a baby, she seldom cried. She was easy to please and generally happy. When she was about a month old, she caught a cold with a terrible cough. The cough usually started during feeding; she would cough until she lost her meal. But then she would stop coughing, look up at the person holding her and deliver a huge smile, as if to say, "Everything's cool. I'm okay now." Britt has not lost this personality trait. She is still easygoing and extroverted, getting along with almost everyone.

My son, the youngest of our kids, is nine at the time of this writing. Although his personality type is not yet set in stone, it is interesting to observe his actions and reactions. It is easy to see that he is a detailed individual who can be quite demanding, although he is polite and easy to get along with. I am not a child psychologist and I don't know whether parents should try to modify their children's personality (I definitely have not delved into this area), but I do know that I can offer advice and guidance to my children. I do this in an attempt help them understand their own personalities and the personalities of others. I try to explain the potential pitfalls as they act and interact with others.

The study of personality styles dates back to the early Greeks. Hippocrates identified four temperaments and referred to them as earth, air, fire, and water. Since then, many studies and methodologies have been developed to measure and classify behavior styles. Today, a number of tests are available to help users define their own behavior style. Some of the best-known tests are the DISC model, the Myers-Briggs evaluation, and the Enneagram. We'll discuss each of these tests later in this chapter.

Why are personality styles important?

What do personality styles show us, and why are they important? Personality styles are not intelligence tests or skill indicators. They do not describe our values, or our personal interests. Personality styles indicate:

- How we prefer to be talked to
- How we can be motivated
- How we prefer to be managed
- What environment we prefer to work in
- What we can contribute to any team or organization
- What our behavioral strengths and weaknesses are
- How we can understand, talk to, motivate, and manage others in the most efficient and effective manner

Personality profiles give users an excellent view of how they function as individuals. This view identifies how they deal with:

- Others
- Stress
- Challenge
- Lack of data
- Decisions
- Action
- Problems
- Power and authority
- Risks
- Supervision
- Socializing
- Teamwork
- Performance
- Listening
- Loyalty
- Details
- Diplomacy
- Accuracy

When you know your personality type, you should be able to paint a good picture of yourself and your Personality Strength Zone. You will be able to identify how to respond in all types of situations. More important, you will know which situations make you the most effective and productive.

The next step in this process is to ensure that you apply this new knowledge, that you place yourself in the proper environment to maximize your effectiveness.

Finally, when you understand yourself and you know how to be more effective, you need to apply this teaching to others in your work environment. By all means, communicate to others what you expect from them as they strive to maximize their effectiveness but, more importantly, when you begin to understand the behavior styles of others, you must ensure that you are communicating and working with the styles of your co-workers in the most effective manner possible. The key is not to expect everyone to bend and adapt to your style, but for you to comply with styles of others in an attempt to make everyone as effective and efficient as possible.

This is important, because no two people are exactly the same. If you treat all people in the same way, your successes will be limited to the small group of people who think like you. However, if you understand that different personality styles prefer to give and receive information and communicate in different ways, and you adapt your communication style to this, you will be much more successful.

What do I mean by this? Let me pose an example. Suppose you were facing a situation where you had to rework a project that was found to be deficient, and you had to get it out the door quickly or you would lose your client. Now suppose that you approach this problem by calling your staff into a meeting and decreeing that everyone must work late and through the weekend, or the company will lose a major client and they might lose their jobs.

How do you suppose the staff members would react? Would everyone react in the same way?

Some people, motivated by a challenge, would immediately start to plan a course of action and begin assigning tasks to people. Some would probably dig in their heels, resisting the pressure tactics. Others would try to focus on the details of what went wrong, attacking the problem at a low level, paralyzed by details and possibly not meeting the deadline. Still others would be totally de-motivated by the pressure, and their production and quality of work would be negatively affected. At best, the end result of your autocratic approach would be disorganized chaos.

Now, what would happen if you approached the problem as follows:

- Call your staff into a conference room and explain the situation in detail, without placing blame or leveling threats

- Assign planning and execution tasks to those who like challenges, who are good at strategy, and who love managing trouble situations

- Assign detail activities to those who love detail tasks, ensuring that they are aware of their exact role and of the impending deadline

- Assign process-related tasks to those who are good at applying pre-defined processes

- Assign tasks that need to be done by more than one person and require a lot of interaction to those who work best in teams

Essentially, if you approached the situation this way you would be identifying each person's Personality Strength Zone and allowing that person to work in his or her own Strength Zone, instead of forcing everyone into your Strength Zone.

Which approach do you think would be more successful?

On Lilongwe, we had many instances where a third party supplied incorrect data that we needed to use for engineering our systems. This was especially inconvenient due to our schedule constraints. Our client was supportive, but wanted our best efforts in fixing the data and incorporating it into our design. We followed up with our design staff, tossing ideas back and forth, assigning tasks to appropriate individuals, and in most cases, coming up with solutions that incorporated the changed data, yet still maintained the schedule.

I have seen the same situation on other projects, however, where the client approached the issue in a totally different manner. I remember one case in particular, in which a third party was late in supplying us with data. The client came at us aggressively, even though the late date was no fault of ours, insisting that the project be re-engineered in a ridiculously short timeframe. This request came with threats, both veiled and unveiled. The client even undermined our management's authority by directly threatening our employees. As you can imagine, this project had a much different outcome than Lilongwe. It was interesting to note that while the client caused a lot of commotion and dissatisfaction on our team (to say the least), their approach caused just as many problems, or more, with their own people.

These examples illustrate why it is important to understand your own personality style and the styles of other people. Without this knowledge, your effectiveness as a person, and as a leader, is compromised.

As Stanley C. Allyn said, "The most useful person in the world today is the man or woman who knows how to get along with other people. Human relations is the most important science in living."

The perfect personality type

There are no perfect personality types. Every personality type, and therefore every person, has strengths and weaknesses. It is important to identify your personality type and to know your strengths and weaknesses. Then you must capitalize on your strengths and ensure that you do not hide behind your weaknesses, using them as an excuse for your behavior or performance.

If you have a dominant personality and like to take charge of every situation, for example, you cannot use this as an excuse to run over others without taking their feelings, ideas, and views into account.

We had a person like this on one of our offshore projects. A technical lead, he had a dominant personality and wanted things done exactly his way all the time. Failure to comply with his dictatorial leadership style often resulted in a screaming tirade. Not only has this individual severely compromised his potential, his behavior has caused a large turnover of staff. Worse yet, management on that project has failed to act. As of this writing the tirades are still happening, and the turnovers continue.

This person will, unfortunately, never be successful. He will never realize his true potential as a person until he takes the time to understand himself, and then takes even more time to understand others. He must then use this understanding to deal fairly and appropriately with every individual on his team.

Similarly, people who are detail-oriented cannot allow themselves to get bogged down in the details of every assignment. Although details may make them happy, being too detail-oriented will not contribute much to the team environment or to the company, especially if assignments are never finished because the work is still being refined to the nth level of perfection. As you can imagine within an engineering environment, we had a number of these individuals within our company. In fact, four of them worked on Lilongwe. Three of them were able, with some coaching, to balance their detail-orientation with the reality of the situation. They produced above-average results with respect to quality and quantity. Unfortunately, the fourth individual had not managed to find this balance and, although extremely knowledgeable, was operating with limited effectiveness. As a result, the person has been refused positions by managers on most projects and will probably end up being "managed" out the door.

The balanced personality

You must not rely on your strengths so much that they become a liability. You have to strive for balance. Even if your strength is logic, do not use logic in situations where compassion is appropriate or the outcome will not be positive. Here's a personal example. When my wife told me about a sweater she had just purchased that got stained, I proceeded to troubleshoot the situation. I tried hard to find a solution, one that would return the sweater to its original condition, but all my wife wanted was a sympathetic ear. The conversation quickly ended when Kelly asked how I thought I could help when I had never washed a load of laundry in my life!

Strive for balance between your strengths and weaknesses. Many of the weaknesses associated with a personality type are due to the dominant characteristic being allowed to dominate the personality. The other personality aspects become subservient to the dominating aspect. This results in an unbalanced personality. It is common in people who go through periods of intense stress.

A good analogy would be a company CEO who is more of a dictator than a balanced leader and who is focused on one aspect of his business, such as operating profit. His focus on operating profit becomes so intense that he ignores his:

- Operations director when told that cutting wages to improve the bottom line is resulting in a mass exodus of human resources from the company

- Sales manager when told that cutting sales positions and sales budgets is only a short-term, bottom-line fix that will have disastrous results in the long term

- Public relations director when told that cutting charitable funding of community events could cause a public boycott of company products

This CEO will wake up one morning to find his company in ruins. But a balanced CEO would take a much different approach to increasing operating profit. He would listen to the operations director, sales manager, and public relations director. Together, they would come up with strategies to increase the bottom-line numbers without destroying the company.

In the same way, people with balanced personalities will resist the urge to let their response to everything in life be dominated by one personality trait. Instead, they recognize when other personality traits should be used, and they follow through with a balanced approach. They also ensure that they are interacting with other people based on the other person's personality type, not based on their personality type.

Essentially, people with balanced personalities balance their Personality Strength Zone with those of their co-workers, thus maximizing the team's effectiveness.

Personality profile goals

A balanced personality is the ultimate goal of the personality profile. When you discover your personality strengths and weaknesses, you can concentrate on your strengths by putting yourself in roles or situations where those strengths can be used effectively. But here's a caution: Do not rely on these strengths to the point that they become your response to everything, and do not ignore your weaknesses. Use a balanced approach to every situation and determine which personality traits are most appropriate for the situation.

Understand that all people are not the same as you are. All people are unique, and all people must be treated differently. You must learn how to read or understand people as individuals and then treat people appropriately, based on their personality types.

When the DISC personality profile tool was introduced in our Calgary workplace, it had a profound impact. Everyone involved immediately began studying personality types in an attempt to understand themselves and their interactions with others. They also studied the other personality types to learn how to deal efficiently with them. People were comparing their personality types in meetings, during lunch, in the coffee areas and around the water cooler. We talked for weeks about how relationship issues that we had struggled with for years were now beginning to make sense.

The underlying goal was to understand that all people are not the same. Every person is unique, and all people cannot be treated the same way. To maximize everyone's performance you must learn how to read and understand people as individuals, and then treat them appropriately. This can be summed up as follows:

The goal of personality profile training is to balance your Personality Strength Zone with the Personality Strength Zone of those you interact with, in an effort to maximize the efficiency and effectiveness of you and those around you.

We learned that our company had a disproportionate number of dominant individuals (D types in the DISC profile). This began to make sense, based on past history. Our owner liked to hire people who could go to a client's site, perform a site survey, provide the client with a list of areas to improve plant performance, provide an estimate to complete this service, implement this service, and come home with a check in hand.

We also had competitions between each personality type. Refereed by our HR group, these competitions included activities such as:

- Defining personality types by the use of flashcards showing key words

- Role-playing to show how we would handle situations with different personality types

- Reviewing training videos and identifying the personality types of the actors

These competitions provided additional training for all involved and allowed the participants to apply their newly acquired knowledge and tools to real life situations. This is truly the key to it all. The new knowledge must be practiced and applied if there is going to be any value extracted.

Personality profile tools

Three of the most popular personality profile techniques are the DISC model, the Myers Briggs model, and the Enneagram. These techniques are described in this chapter, with the most time spent on the DISC profile, as it is my preferred tool due to, among other things, its simplicity. However, before we look at these profile tools, let's briefly examine a simple, but effective, profile description provided by Zig Ziglar in his book, *Top Performance*.

Zig Ziglar's model

Ziglar defines his personality profile model as having four components:

1.　Aggression
2.　People skills
3.　Patience
4.　Quality

He describes each of these components, comparing them to a vessel being filled to a line that is either below, or above, the midline. He also describes how to motivate people within each component type. This is summarized as follows:

Aggression

When the aggression component is below midline, the person is generally quiet and unassuming, mild-mannered and modest. He or she is willing to let others make the decisions or decisions are made by consensus. Often, these people can be taken advantage of by others. You can motivate these people by placing them in low-pressure situations, or by adopting a let's-do-it-together style of leadership. Incentive motivation does not work, as they do not like pressure.

When the aggression component is above midline, the person is typically a strong-willed, task-oriented doer who drives himself or herself, and others, hard. These people enjoy challenge and change. They can easily become workaholics, with a lack of attention to detail and abrasive personalities. You can motivate these people by challenging them and by granting them authority. When disagreeing with them, stick with facts – don't attack the person. They are pioneers, not followers.

People skills

People who have below-midline people skills are willing to spend time without others around. For that reason, they may be perceived as aloof. Typically, they are slow to speak out, and they may be suspicious of others. To motivate these people, provide a work environment that is free from social contracts. Allow them to think out problems by themselves – they are best at logical analysis. They do not like loud people, or being forced to solve people problems.

People with above-midline people skills are spontaneous, enthusiastic, friendly, and good at persuading others to join them. They make decisions using their hearts, rather than their minds. They are poised, relaxed, charming, emotional, and optimistic. In fact, they may be more concerned with popularity than with work. They can be guilty of overselling and of avoiding problems. To motivate them, give them time to socialize, to express ideas and opinions. They don't like intense concentration or record keeping, and they don't like criticism of friends.

Patience

Below-midline performers prefer an unstructured environment. They invite change and are frustrated by the status quo. Impulsive, excitable initiators, they may be anxious, nervous, or tense. They must be made to finish what they start. Motivate these people by giving them a variety of activities and by giving them freedom on jobs.

People who are above the midline in the patience department prefer a structured environment. They are stable, kind, patient, quiet, disciplined, service-oriented, hardworking individuals who typically listen to others and are friendly, relaxed, loyal, sincere, dependable team players. They are turned off by pressure, by new tasks, and by being forced to initiate new projects. Motivate these people by giving them time to adjust, and by introducing no surprises and few changes. Show appreciation for their completed tasks.

Quality

When it comes to quality, people operating at a below-midline level are generally strong-willed, independent, and quantity-oriented. Motivate them by granting autonomy, but be sure to include a Q&A guideline or a Q&A step.

Above-midline people are conscientious, with a concern for detail. They are intuitive, competent, accurate thinkers who are uncomfortable showing emotion and who may over-analyze situations because they do not like making quick decisions. Motivate these people by giving them personal attention, and by giving them an exact job description within a controlled work environment.

Although Zig Ziglar's model may seem quite simple, it is effective in describing different personality types. As you read through it, it is easy to begin to classify yourself as either above or below the midpoint in each category. If you spend some time reviewing it, you can begin to place work associates and acquaintances into the appropriate category. Once you are able to do this, the next step is to apply the appropriate motivators, as defined by this model, to yourself, and to others. This will help you to maximize your own efficiency, as well as the efficiency of those around you.

For more details, see Zig Ziglar's book *Top Performance* (listed in the Resources section at the back of this book).

Riso-Hudson Enneagram Type Indicator (RHETI)

Although the Ziglar model is useful in trying to appreciate the difference between personalities, it does not have as much science behind it as the Enneagram, and it does not come with a profile tool that allows users to determine where they fit within Ziglar's personality spectrum.

The Enneagram personality profile developed by Don Richard Riso and Russ Hudson is based on the concept that everyone is a combination of nine distinct personality types:

1. **Reformer – rational, idealistic type:** principled, purposeful, self-controlled, and perfectionist

2. **Helper – caring, interpersonal type:** demonstrative, generous, people-pleasing, and possessive

3. **Achiever – success-oriented, pragmatic type:** adaptive, excelling, driven, and image-conscious

4. **Individualist – sensitive, withdrawn type:** expressive, dramatic, self-absorbed, and temperamental

5. **Investigator – intense, cerebral type:** perceptive, innovative, secretive, and isolated

6. **Loyalist – committed, security-oriented type:** engaging, responsible, anxious, and suspicious

7. **Enthusiast – busy, fun-loving type:** spontaneous, versatile, distractible, and scattered

8. **Challenger – powerful, dominating type:** self-confident, decisive, willful, and confrontational

9. **Peacemaker – easy-going, self-effacing type:** receptive, reassuring, agreeable, and complacent

The profile tool is available online at www.enneagraminstitute.com at a cost of $10 (U.S.). The tool consists of one hundred forty-four pairs of statements in a forced-choice format. It takes approximately forty minutes to complete. When you have completed the test, the online tool immediately provides your results. According to Enneagram Institute research, everyone has one dominant personality type, with a number of sub-dominant types or "wings." The profile tool also identifies the personality type scored lowest by the user – indicating an area of potential weakness that needs to be addressed, or at least understood.

The resulting profile and analysis provided online is great, but if you really want to understand the model, and the theory behind it, you need to purchase *Discovering Your Personality Type*, a book by Don Richard Riso and Russ Hudson. Links to purchase the book are available on the website. The book can be bought at most bookstores, including Amazon. I believe this is an excellent tool, although I also think it is more complicated to understand than the DISC profile.

My profile results from the free version of the test returned a personality of Challenger, described as a "powerful, dominating type, self-confident, decisive, willful, and confrontational." I found the pages of analysis that came with this free test quite valuable. Summaries for the Challenger profile were categorized as Healthy Challenger, At Their Best Challenger, Average Challenger, and Unhealthy Challenger. I found this information to be very useful.

Also provided was a key motivation section for the Challenger, listing the motivators for this personality type. Then came an interesting section with profiles of famous people with this personality type. Martin Luther King, Jr. and Sean Connery both have the same profiles as me!

Finally, a complete, in-depth overview of the Challenger type provided a detailed look at problem areas that Challengers may run into.

Note that the Enneagram tool was independently validated in 2001 by Rebecca Newgent, PhD. Refer to the website for more details on the study by Newgent and for additional web links on her study.

Myers Briggs

The Myers Briggs profile tool is similar to the Enneagram, in that a lot of study and research has been invested in it. Myers Briggs requires each person to complete the profiling booklet, which can be purchased online at a number of sites. Links are available at www.StrengthZone.ca and most profiles can be purchased for about $60US. However, I recommend that you use the DISC profile rather than the Myers Briggs. A DISC profile tool has been provided in the next section of this chapter.

The Myers Briggs test was first developed by Isabel Briggs Myers and her mother, Katherine Cook Briggs. It was based on Carl Jung's book, *Psychological Types*. Jung's personality model is based on the following four preferences:

1. Where you direct the majority of your energy
2. How you process information most effectively
3. How you make decisions
4. How you organize your life

According to the Myers Briggs tool, each personality type is assigned a letter indicating the four aspects of his or her personality:

1) Where, primarily, do you direct your energy?

a. To the outer world of activity and spoken words (Extroversion)
b. To the inner world of thoughts and emotions (Introversion)

2) How do you prefer to process information?

a.   In the form of known facts and familiar terms (Sensing)
b.   In the form of possibilities or new potential (iNtuition)

3) How do you prefer to make decisions?

a.   On the basis of logic and objective considerations (Thinking)
b.   On the basis of personal values (Feeling)

4) How do you prefer to organize your life?

a.   In a structured way, making decisions and knowing where you stand (Judgment)
b.   In a flexible way, discovering life as you go along (Perception)

Each of these personality types is assigned a letter:

Letter	Meaning	Area
E	Extroversion	Energy Focus
I	Introversion	Energy Focus
S	Sensing	Information Processing
N	iNtuition	Information Processing
T	Thinking	Decision Making
F	Feeling	Decision Making
J	Judgment	Organization
P	Perception	Organization

Each personality is classified as some combination of the four personality preferences. Because there are four personality preferences and only two choices for each preference, sixteen combinations of letters have been identified as part of the Myers Briggs model. Although everyone is individual and unique, these letter combinations are combined into generalized, similar themes.

 Links to more detailed information and theme descriptions are available at www.StrengthZone.ca.

DISC

Introduction

This section will describe the DISC personality profiling system. As with Myers Briggs and the Enneagram, this system has a better scientific base than the Ziglar model. The DISC system requires each person to complete a profile tool (provided as part of this book by PeopleKeys).

Access the profile on the Internet by going to www.StrengthZone.ca and clicking on the "Take the DISC Profile" link. This will take you to a sign-in screen, where you will have to enter the unique code printed on the inside cover of this book. After entering your code, you will be taken to the online DISC profile. Follow the instructions provided and complete your DISC profile.

Note that before completing the online profile you should read the following information on the DISC profile. It explains the history of DISC and defines the process. The DISC system is based on William Moulton Marston's book, *The Emotions of Normal People*. In this book, he identified four main temperaments: **Dominant, Influential, Steady**, and **Conscientious**. Everyone embodies some combination of these four temperaments. William Clark subsequently took this information and developed a tool that allows people to evaluate themselves, and to gain an understanding of how they and others see the world and respond to that perception. The DISC model is the one that we will spend the most time describing, as I feel that it is the simplest to use and understand.

DISC Model

The DISC model considers two dimensions of personality: introversion versus extraversion and people-focused versus task-focused. Introverted people prefer a supporting role as opposed to one that places them in the spotlight, which is where extroverts prefer to be. Task-focused people prefer to attack the details and get the job done, while people-focused individuals get their jobs done by communicating with people. These two dimensions can be summarized in the following chart.

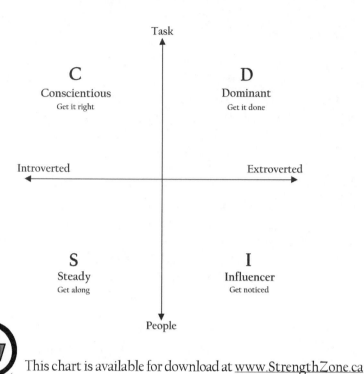

This chart is available for download at www.StrengthZone.ca

All people embody some combination of all of the above personality styles. However, people with similar DISC profiles, or similar personality styles, can still be quite different from each other. This is due to the influence of values, talents, skills, and knowledge, and how they handle their unique strengths and weaknesses. Therefore, the personality profile tools cannot be used as the sole means of determining a person's effectiveness.

A summary of each of the four DISC personality styles in isolation is summarized below.

Dominant	Influencer	Steady	Conscientious
Demanding	Persuasive	Consistent	Adheres to standards
Action-oriented	Enthusiastic	Doesn't like change	Concentrates on details
Direct	Entertaining	Patient	Analytical
Domineering	People person	Loyal	Systematic
Forceful	Social	Helps others	Analyzes performance
Risk-taker	Group work	Stable	Highly accurate

A more detailed look at each personality type can be found in the following tables:

 These tables are available for download at
www.StrengthZone.ca

"D" personalities

Dominant – People with this type of personality are task-oriented and tend to shape their environment by overcoming opposition to accomplish the desired results.

Tendencies	<ul><li>Wants immediate results - impatient</li><li>Loves challenge</li><li>Very competitive</li><li>Initiates action</li><li>Confident</li><li>Risk-taker</li><li>Makes snap decisions but can change a decision when new data comes in</li><li>Questions popular thinking</li><li>Takes authority</li><li>Solves problems</li><li>Manages trouble</li><li>Task oriented</li></ul>
Required work environment	<ul><li>Authority</li><li>Power</li><li>Frequent and new challenges</li><li>Individual accomplishment</li><li>Wide scope of operations</li><li>Direct answers</li><li>Freedom from controls or supervision</li><li>Ability to advance or be promoted</li><li>Varied activities</li><li>Independence</li></ul>
Needs people who	<ul><li>Review pros and cons of decisions</li><li>Are cautious in decision making and calculate risks</li><li>Have empathy towards others</li></ul>
To be more effective	<ul><li>Must have challenging work</li><li>Must pace themselves and relax</li><li>Must understand that they need others</li><li>Must take the time required for decisions and must try to have enough data to make the proper decision</li></ul>
Major strengths	<ul><li>Efficient organizers</li><li>Focused</li><li>Results oriented</li><li>Responsible for actions and decisions</li></ul>
Major limitations	<ul><li>Lack of people skills</li><li>Making decisions without all of the information required</li></ul>
Dealing with D types	<ul><li>Start with the bottom line</li><li>Look for mutual areas of agreement (mutual wins)</li><li>Don't lead up to the task at hand with small talk Get to the point</li><li>Ask "What" questions not "How" questions</li><li>Stick to facts, not opinion</li><li>Don't over-dominate</li><li>Don't patronize</li><li>Be prepared and organized</li><li>Be clear and direct</li></ul>

We have all seen and experienced a high D sometime in our lives. Chances are that you have at least one or more in your place of work. At work, high Ds bulldoze their way through everything and everybody. In his book *The Fred Factor*, Mark Sanborn describes a high D weakness when he states that "Transactional interactions focus primarily on results, sometimes even at the cost of relationships. People who value results over relationships are often called 'direct.' That means they go directly for the outcome, making others feel devalued and even used."

High Ds cannot wait for results. Results must be immediate, and everyone must be heading in the same direction at breakneck speed. These people can rally the troops and get things done quickly and efficiently, but due to their lack of people skills they tend to leave a trail of casualties behind them. General Patton is an example of a high D, as the following extracts illustrate:

Patton was unquestionably the outstanding exponent of armored warfare produced by the Allies in the Second World War. In terms of blood and iron, he personified the national genius, which had raised the United States from humble beginnings to world power: the eagerness to seize opportunities and to exploit them to the full, the ruthless overriding of opposition, the love of the unconventional, the ingenious and the unorthodox, the will to win whatever the cost and above all, in the shortest possible time.

- H. Essame's Patton: The Commander

On the Lilongwe project, I did not have to look far to find high Ds. I only had to look in the mirror every morning. I can think of multiple situations during our weekly project review meetings where someone would indicate that progress was being held up due to what I thought was unacceptable performance by one or more individuals. In these instances, I would approach the problem like a typical D – like a bull in a china shop. However, I had a number of excellent technical leads who would remind me of the ramifications of actions taken in haste. For the most part, they were able to straighten me out before I acted rashly.

One technical lead would dish out tasks to her team members but then constantly check on progress. Most of the time, the tasks would require days or weeks to complete, but the lead would check in with her team members multiple times a day to determine progress. Her personality profile was a D followed by a C – not only was she domineering and wanting immediate results, but she was also very focused on the details. Most of her team members quickly grew quite tired of this continual bombardment. The Ds perceived her as assaulting their need for autonomy, the Is saw her behavior as too serious (it was not a fun environment), the S types, who hate conflict, cringed every time she came by, and the Cs began to view her as incompetent. It became almost a full-scale mutiny, until I realized what was happening and sat down with the lead to explain how her behavior was negatively impacting the team.

———————

"I" personalities

Influence – People with this type of personality are people-focused and interactive. They shape their environment by influencing others to accomplish desired results.

Tendencies	• Interacting with people • Working in a group • Being optimistic about circumstances and people • Articulate • Making a good impression • Creating enthusiasm • Entertaining people • Impulsive • Inspirational • Excitable • Persuasive • Trusting
Required work environment	• An environment with recognition socially and recognition of ability • People-focused or interactive • Free from detail and overburdening controls • Where they are free to express themselves
Needs people who	• Concentrate on activities • Deal with things instead of people • Take a logical and/or systematic approach
To be more effective	• Provide recognition • Requires help with time management • Help them set priorities • Freedom to achieve the end result without overbearing rules • Friendly work environment
Major strengths	• Optimistic • Persuasive • Helping others • Flexible • Negotiating • Motivating • Enthusiastic • Manage change well
Major limitations	• Time management • Too emotional • May be sarcastic • Not a good finisher • Impulsive
Dealing with I types	• Listen to them • Start on a social note and move into business • Be friendly • Expect fast decisions but ask questions to confirm the legitimacy of the decision • Recognize them in public but never criticize them in public • Ask for their input

Everyone loves an I, and I personalities love interacting with other people. They strive to make a good impression and are the life of the party. Excitable and inspirational, they are easily distracted from the task at hand, but they do their best work as part of a group or team. This is where their interaction skills can be maximized. They are good negotiators, and they love to help others. They love public recognition, but they must never be criticized in public.

A high-profile example of an I personality is Ronald Reagan. Reagan was well-known for his easygoing and cheerful attitude. He built and maintained personal relationships with all of his staff members.

Reagan's popularity survived concern over economic and other policy matters, for he possessed a leadership style that stressed inspiration over management.

- From Grolier Multimedia Encyclopedia – by Otis L. Graham, Jr.

Ronald Reagan displayed consistent optimism and a jaunty self-confidence that endeared him to millions.

- From Encyclopedia Americana – by Robert J. Huckshorn

The only high I personalities on Lilongwe were on the sales team and among the document control staff. The engineering staff was too serious and too focused to be I types. It was always interesting to watch the engineering team open up and have fun in social functions to which the I people were invited. When only Ds and Cs attend, our business unit meetings can be quite boring.

"S" personalities
Steadiness – People with this type of personality are pragmatic and practical. They shape their environment by cooperating with others within existing circumstances to complete tasks.

Tendencies	• Stability • Good listeners • Patient and tolerant • Logical • Harmony – does not like conflict • Perform consistently • Helps others • Develops specialized skills • Creates a stable environment
Required work environment	• Where sincere appreciation is provided for work performed • Requires process and time to finish work • Acceptance • Maintenance of environment without change • Predictable routines • Standard operating procedures • Minimal conflict
Needs people who	• Handle unexpected change • Handle conflict • Are flexible • Who can apply pressure to others when required
To be more effective	• Needs appreciation • Consistency • Clear direction • Must be conditioned before change occurs • Must know how his or her effort contributes • Must have creativity encouraged
Major strengths	• Tolerant • Patient • Loyal • Team player • Dependable • Supportive • Manages repetitive work • Practical and organized
Major limitations	• Under stress can become stubborn and not want to negotiate • Sudden change • Indecisive • Oversensitive • Holds a grudge • Does not like dealing with conflict
Dealing with S types	• Provide sufficient detail • Be sincere • Provide time for decisions • Reduce risk

Strength Zone

High S personalities are the people you can rely on in a stable environment to consistently deliver results. S types are patient and tolerant, which makes them good listeners. They like to help others. They do not like unexpected changes, as they are comfortable with processes and procedures that they know and understand. They thrive at handling repetitive activities, but avoid conflict at all costs.

The people working in the accounting department on the Lilongwe project were mostly high S personalities. They were great, dependable people who were willing to work overtime and to do whatever it took to get the accounting tasks completed. They were classic high S people.

Toward the end of the Lilongwe project, however, our top finance people decided to replace our accounting system, called Solomon, with a product that Oracle sold. This project was no small undertaking. It would have to be an all-or-nothing approach to transferring the data between the two systems. One day, they were using Solomon, and the next day, they would be using Oracle. This meant that at the time of the transfer, they would have to have all of their projects up to date – and we knew that several projects were many months behind.

As the "go live" date approached, I watched our accounting group, facing two types of stress, begin to withdraw. First, they were trying to get an enormous amount of work completed in an impossibly short timeframe. Second, they were switching to an unknown, untried accounting system. Their current processes and procedures were no longer valid.

The result was that the accounting staff became overwhelmed with the workload. Some were unable to even determine their top priorities. To cope, I brought in additional staff to offload the workload and to allow the permanent staff to refocus and properly prioritize their work.

"C" personalities

Conscientiousness – People with this type of personality stress results and processes or methods. They shape their environment by working conscientiously within existing circumstances to ensure quality and accuracy.

Tendencies	• Compliant • Competent • Analytical thinkers • Try to improve everything • Adhere to standards • Diplomatic • Uses indirect approaches to conflict • Uses systematic approach to situations
Required work environment	• Clearly defined expectations • Quality • Reserved atmosphere • Demonstrate expertise • Recognition for skills and accomplishments • Opportunity to get to details
Needs people who	• Delegate • Make quick decisions • Treat policies as guidelines • Initiate and facilitate discussions • Encourage teamwork
To be more effective	• Sufficient time • Information • Low risk environment • Details and procedure
Major strengths	• Analytical • Perfectionist • Quality • Very organized • Attention to detail • Cautious • Logical and task focused
Major limitations	• Judgmental • Narrow focus • Fear of criticism of work causes too much focus on detail • May withdraw under stress and focus on small details • Not flexible • Over analysis
Dealing with C types	• Be patient • Be organized and respectful of their time • Provide supporting details • Be clear in your answers • Stay calm and logical when they question • Minimize risk • Use open ended questions

High Cs are stereotyped as Mr. Spock or Commander Data from Star Trek. Cs are extremely detailed, analytical thinkers who show little or no emotion. Every activity and decision is logically thought out and systematically analyzed. They are perfectionists who tend to spend more time on activities than others feel is necessary. However, they are ensuring that what they complete is absolutely perfect. They are very organized and very cautious. They will not make snap decisions, and they require time to answer questions. They can be inflexible, as their analytical nature opposes all solutions and processes except solutions that are perfect.

A high-profile example of a C would be Bill Gates or Albert Einstein.

On Lilongwe, we had a number of high C people, as you would expect in an engineering company. We found that these people worked best in the background, doing detailed programming according to predefined technical specifications and only interfacing with our client when discussion on purely technical issues was required. We found that we would encounter issues when we put the Cs in a role where they had to routinely interface with the client. These incidents were usually caused by the client interrupting the C at work too many times (possibly only once). The C would then make a rude comment or display an inappropriate attitude toward the client.

We had one of our C type engineers working in northern Canada at a gas plant startup. He was extremely intelligent and very experienced. When I visited the gas plant some months after the successful startup, one of the operators asked, "Do you still have that engineer working for you who just turns and stares at you as if you were stupid when you ask him a question?" Apparently, this individual would answer a question once, but if asked the same question a second time, even for clarification, he would just turn and stare at the asker, then return to work without replying. Consequently, we moved this person to a technical position that did not require much client interaction.

How it works

As explained earlier, the DISC system considers two dimensions of personality – introversion versus extraversion and people-focused versus task-focused. The method used to determine where you fit between these two dimensions is the DISC personality profile system. Most DISC systems that I am familiar with get the user to rate themselves against a series of twenty-four to thirty four-word combinations. The user has to pick one of the four as *Most Like Me* and one of the four as *Least Like Me*. This is usually done in the context of how the user perceives himself or herself at work, not how others might perceive the user.

Once the user moves through these twenty-four to thirty four-word combinations, the resulting data is used to build three bar chart graphs similar to the one shown below.

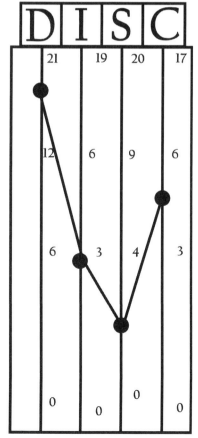

The first chart graphs the *Most Like* score, the second chart graphs the *Least Like* score, and the third chart graphs the difference between them. This third chart is your resultant personality profile graph. The graphing techniques including the statistics and mathematics are beyond the scope of this document – although I'd love to go into detail here.

Everyone has a unique personality, regardless of their DISC profile, but some typical DISC profiles have been identified, and these descriptions are available online. Also, most DISC profile systems classify a person by their two highest plots on the overall personality profile graph. For example, the graph shown above is my profile. I would be known as a D-C, where D is my primary style and C is my secondary style.

Combinations

Note that my profile in the graph above is described as a Challenger, as defined in the profile descriptions available online. The exact title of the profile depends on the manufacturer of the DISC tool.

As discussed with previous models, no one is strictly limited to one personality type. Everyone is a combination of D, I, S, and C. According to the DISC model, the most common combinations of these four personality profiles have been identified and are available online as part of the personality profile exercise.

Additional uses

The techniques taught in the DISC profile tool have many uses but what it boils down to is that each person needs to strive to understand and interact with others more efficiently. What you will find is that with practice, this becomes a lot easier. For example, after much study, I am now usually able to judge what a person's primary and secondary DISC style is within a half hour interview with that person. I use this information to determine whether that person will fit into a particular team.

As an example, here is a story about an individual who I'll call Jack. A number of years ago, before we established training programs similar to those outlined in this book, I began receiving complaints from members of our project accounting group about Jack's behavior. It seemed that Jack was under an extreme workload. He was putting in long hours and had not taken a full weekend off in months. The harder Jack worked, the further he fell behind, and the more stressed he became. Jack would show up at the desks of his co-workers, demanding assistance because his project was more important. Not only was Jack's demeanor unprofessional, in a number of cases, he reduced his co-workers to tears.

I sat down with Jack and we talked about these incidents. Jack agreed they had taken place. He was willing to take responsibility for them and to make amends. Although we had been through the DISC process, we hadn't dedicated a lot of time or effort to implementing the processes. As we talked about the DISC profiles, I learned that Jack was a D-C, which means he can be direct and blunt, even to the point of being rude. Stress can amplify this behavior.

Jack and I discussed other methods of interacting with people. He said he would try to temper his approach, and I agreed to offload some of his work. However, I didn't schedule a follow-up meeting.

Predictably, everything went smoothly for a few months, but soon, I began hearing more whispers about Jack and then a few substantial complaints. I called him into my office again. In the first instance, he had been aware that his actions had caused issues, whereas this time, he was not aware of the problems. In the meantime, I had learned a great deal more about the DISC methodology and about the value of using the DISC principles. Jack's lack of awareness about the inappropriateness of his actions was caused by his lack of attention to others. As a typical D-C, he was so focused on his own world that he was unaware of how he was interacting with others, and how unproductive and even damaging this behavior was. Clearly, the situation now was more serious.

Because Jack was an extremely valuable employee, one who was capable of greater work production with greater accuracy than many of his peers, I had a huge vested interest in getting him back on track. My approach was to review his DISC profile again, re-emphasizing that his type can be direct and abrasive and stressing that just knowing this was not good enough – Jack had to be conscious of his potential to act in this fashion. He absolutely needed to tailor his responses to others in a professional and courteous manner, showing respect for those with whom he was interacting.

We didn't stop there. I encouraged Jack to spend time with the DISC material so that eventually he was able to accurately determine the DISC profiles of his co-workers and to interact with them in the most efficient manner possible for *them*, not for himself.

After this conversation, Jack said he wanted to get together on a weekly basis to discuss his progress and hear about any additional feedback from his co-workers that I may have received. I am happy to say that at the time of this writing, Jack still seems to be getting along just fine with his co-workers.

The lesson this experience taught me is that it is imperative not to let your guard down but to continue to watch your interactions with others, ensuring that you are interacting in the most efficient manner possible for the *other* person, not for yourself.

In his book *Courageous Leadership*, Bill Hybels says that when you are hiring people, you need to consider character, competency, and chemistry. Character was discussed in the last chapter on values. Competency is the application of skills, knowledge, and talents, which will be discussed later in this book. Chemistry is essentially personality or the fit between personalities. Personality fit is extremely important when hiring someone into an existing team. Hiring the wrong personality type and placing the person on a team can result in devastating clashes. Conversely, hiring the correct personality type can lead to the team gelling and interacting positively, efficiently, and productively.

Conclusion

Learning about and understanding personality types is not an exact science. Before you can become proficient at it you will have to:

1. Study the personality profile tools and profile descriptions.

2. Identify your Personality Strength Zone.

3. Practice listening intently and sincerely.

4. Practice applying your personality profile knowledge and skills.

Always attempt to deal appropriately within the other person's Personality Strength Zone. In doing this, you will be working toward becoming the person that Stanley C. Allyn calls "the most useful person in the world." You will possess the ability that John D. Rockefeller would pay more for "than for any under the sun."

Summary

1. Personality profiles are important because they indicate how we function as individuals and they allow us to understand how we can best interact (efficiently, effectively, and productively) with other people.

2. There is no such thing as the perfect personality.

3. Every person must strive for a balanced personality.

4. The goal of the personality profile is to allow individuals to ensure that their personality is as balanced as possible.

5. Complete and study your DISC profile as per the instructions below:

The profile can be accessed on the Internet by going to www.StrengthZone.ca and clicking on the "Take the DISC Profile" button. This will take you to a sign-in screen where you will be able to enter the unique code found printed on the inside cover of this book. Note that only one DISC profile is available per book.

Application exercise

1. Draw your DISC graph below.

2. What is your DISC profile?

3. List six to eight key words that best define your DISC profile. This can be taken from your DISC profile description provided with your test results. This is your Personality Strength Zone.

1	
2	
3	
4	
5	
6	
7	
8	

4. Pick three acquaintances and based on your DISC knowledge, guess their two primary DISC attributes. List them in the chart below.

	Name	DISC Guess	DISC Actual
1			
2			
3			

5. Have them take the DISC evaluation (as per the instructions earlier in this chapter) and record the results in the chart above. How close were you in your evaluation of these people?

6. Can you see how your personality differences or similarities can react negatively with your "test group" above? List some examples.

7. Can you see how your personality differences or similarities can react positively with your "test group" above? List some examples.

8. How can you change the way that you interact with these people to enhance your relationship and to work more productively together? List examples.

9. Can you identify other relationships that you need to work on using the DISC knowledge that you have gained through this exercise? Who are they, what are their DISC profiles, and what changes do you need to make in your relationship with these individuals?

Personality Profiles of Others

· 4 ·

The greatest ability in business is to get along with others and influence their actions. A chip on the shoulder is too heavy a piece of baggage to carry through life.

- John Hancock

No matter how much work a man can do, no matter how engaging his personality may be, he will not advance far in business if he cannot work through others.

- John Craig

The ability to recognize personality types in others, and to adjust your communication style to match theirs, is vitally important to your success. This chapter presents a number of techniques that can help you determine another person's personality type just by observing key visual and verbal clues.

First: a caution. Although the techniques and tips in this chapter are helpful and useful, you should be aware that this is a complex topic. Many external factors can cause you to jump to the wrong conclusion. For the purpose of clarity, I will be describing individuals who are exceptionally strong in one area of their personality profile – a high D, for example, but every person embodies a combination of all four DISC types of personality, and few individuals will exactly fit the personality molds described in this chapter.

In your own sphere, I encourage you to think of this as a process of identifying the personality type of others through intense observation, as opposed to an instantaneous decision machine. If you spend time studying the DISC profiles, using the information provided in this chapter and practicing the techniques as often as possible, in my experience, the top two DISC styles of a person can usually be fairly accurately determined.

The two main methods I use in determining a person's personality style are visual clues and verbal clues. Visual clues include things like clothing style, hairstyle, car, house décor, and office décor, while verbal clues obviously relate to how a person communicates verbally.

Visual clues

Although visual clues might seem to be the easiest to use in identifying personality types because they are out there for everyone to see, they can also be quite deceptive. Not every person is an island. Most people, in fact, are not. Most men have a woman in their lives who assists them with clothing purchases, hairstyles, choice of vehicles, house décor, and office décor. Similarly, most women have a man who influences their appearance. Likewise, the media influences everyone. Some people even go as far as hiring fashion consultants, interior designers, and architects to help them create a calculated visual appearance. Visual appearances can assist you in determining someone's personality style, but close observation is also required. Don't jump to conclusions.

Verbal clues

When I spend half an hour with someone in an interview situation, I ask many questions. I also listen intently not only to the answers, but to *how* the person answers. The questions I ask are not secret personality-determining trigger questions; they are just simple questions that need answering for me to determine a person's technical qualifications. The trick is to listen carefully to *how* the person answers. These are verbal clues.

I find that verbal clues are the most accurate in determining personality styles. The reason is that personality is always on display. It is difficult for someone to fake his or her personality for any length of time. The only exceptions are Hollywood actors, who are able to get into character before filming starts and stay in character until the scene ends. The actors are often much different than the characters they are portraying, yet they can convince audiences that they are real. However, the vast majority of people cannot do this. I suppose that's why actors and actresses in Hollywood get paid exorbitant amounts of money.

Most people wear their personalities on their shirtsleeves. They may be able to fake things for awhile, but their true styles will soon become apparent.

Over the next few pages, you will find descriptions of how individuals with high D, I, S, and C personalities typically appear and communicate in public. Worksheets summarizing these traits are provided at the end of the chapter. Use these worksheets in interviews, meetings, or other situations to help you identify the personality styles of others. These sheets can also be found at www.StrengthZone.ca.

As you read through these descriptions, visualize encounters that you have had with friends, family members, co-workers, and even strangers. See if you can determine their personality styles.

"D" personalities

People with D personalities like to travel light. They will typically bring a small briefcase or portfolio folder to a job interview, and they will bring a simple notebook to a meeting, if that. I have known Ds to show up at a meeting with no notebook or pen and then borrow some paper and a pen to take notes. I worked with a client a number of years ago, who did not take any notes at any meetings. He insisted that he could remember everything and that note-taking was not required. He was a strong D who actually ended up flaming out rather dramatically after he lost track of the many details on his project. Remember from the last chapter – you have to know your strengths and weaknesses and take a balanced approach, or at some point you will fail.

Ds go on international trips with small carry-on suitcases. They do not need much luggage, as they bring only the essentials. They hate checking bags because they do not have control over this process. They have no problem, however, rearranging the luggage of other passengers in the aircraft's overhead bins to make room for their own luggage near their seat. They don't think twice about telling people what they think about the service on a plane, in a restaurant, in a store, or wherever. They are up-front, bold risk-takers, but they can also be pushy, abrasive, rude, and obnoxious, especially when under stress.

When Ds go shopping, they have a well-defined agenda. It is quite typical for Ds to have detailed shopping lists. They do not window shop. They know the stores where they have to go, and they may even know the item's exact location in the store. They typically will not drive from one store to another looking for the best price, as this wastes their time. If given an opportunity, they will barter vigorously over price, and they will walk away from a deal if the price is not where they feel it should be. Typically, Ds walk into the store, buy the item they need, and leave.

Being a high D myself, I know these shopping patterns very well. Each year at Christmas I ask my wife to give me some gift suggestions. I take these items and make a list, which I then categorize based on availability per store. I then go out directly to the identified stores and buy everything on the list, spending as little time in the mall as possible. Some years, I have been able to buy everything on my list at one department store (at a premium price, I am sure) in less than twenty minutes. That's shopping! However, I'm told (by the highest of authorities – my wife and daughters) that it is a callous and cold way to shop for someone you love, so over the years, I have been trying to change. Whenever I spend "quality" time window-shopping, however, I really do find it draining.

Ds will have high-level resumes that are direct and to the point. As an interviewer, you may have to ask for more detail. Ds tend to communicate in short, precise, to-the-point memos and emails that come complete with bulleted lists, but little detail.

When you walk into a Ds office you will typically see a well-organized, businesslike, almost stark environment, with everything filed neatly and only work that is currently in progress on the desktop.

**Good example of an office of a D type individual. Note the
relatively clean desktop and bare walls
(this person takes their laptop home at night).**

As previously noted, however, a person's office may not be a good
indicator if someone else has spruced things up. My wife, for example,
comes in and hangs my degree, plaques, awards, and pictures, so my
office looks like it is inhabited by an I.

Most Ds are conservative dressers. They typically dress neatly and
distinctly, but have to be forced to wear anything trendy or flashy.

With respect to verbal clues, Ds are typically extroverts. They are
known for their direct, no-nonsense, to-the-point speaking style. They
tend to be commanding speakers who focus on their own objectives in
conversations. Keep in mind that they are much more task-oriented
than people-oriented. As such, they typically talk more about activities
and results than about people. They also talk more about individual
accomplishments than about team accomplishments. They can be
frustrated by lack of action, and in some circumstances, they may become

"rammy" – trying to push through their own agenda and force action. For this reason, I call Ds bulldozers.

Ds prefer to take lead roles. They like to be in control. They do not like wordy questions or explanations, and they are not shy about asking speakers to get to the point. They are typically poor listeners, as they mentally move on to something else if the other person takes too long to make a point. Although they may not go out of their way to find these situations, they do not back away from high-risk, high-stress, and high-conflict situations. They can perform well under these circumstances, but if they are under too much stress, they can also revert to bulldozer behavior.

Ds prefer to deal with concepts, rather than details. They want to leave the details for others. They will nail down the concept at a high level and then pass the project onto someone else so that they can move onto the next concept. They can be stimulated into action by asking "What if" questions. They typically ask "What" questions.

Ds also prefer to communicate with, or through, metaphors and analogies. They relate best to mental pictures. If you are trying to run an idea or concept past them, try a metaphor or an analogy.

"I" personalities

Someone with an I personality might bring a briefcase to a job interview and a notebook or computer to a business meeting. However, I personalities probably won't use much of what they bring. That's because I types prefer to talk and interact with others. They may take a few notes and doodle a few pictures, but they will spend most of their time interacting. They prefer that others complete written communication, as this can be tedious and boring.

I types go on international trips with small carry-on suitcases or, depending on their mood, with large suitcases. They have no problem checking bags, as long as they can talk to people as the bags are being checked and to other passengers as they are waiting at the baggage carousel after the flight. On the airplane, they will strike up conversations with everyone around them, passengers and crew alike. They tend to be upbeat, optimistic, and trusting of others.

A few years ago, I met a high I person while I was traveling. As the plane was boarding on a flight between Knoxville and Denver, a Japanese lady sat down next to me. I was in the window seat and trapped. She immediately tried to strike up a conversation, but it quickly became apparent that she did not speak much English. However, this did not stop her. She was polite but relentless. All I wanted to do was sit back and read my book – at the time I was reading *The Tipping Point* by Malcolm Gladwell, aptly titled, as on that flight, I came close to tipping into insanity. All she wanted to do was to try speaking English. By the time we arrived in Denver, I had taught her about twenty-five new words and explained, using basic words, sign language, and drawings, where I lived, what I did for a living, who I married, and the names and ages of my kids. She had exuberantly reciprocated, using her own basic words, sign language, and drawings, that she was on vacation with her only daughter and that she had a son and husband back in Japan. She was most definitely an I!

I types go shopping for fun. They typically go with a few friends and have no problem striking up conversations with strangers they meet while shopping. They love to browse and can spend hours shopping with seemingly no progress toward any purchase, although they can also be impulse buyers. I people hold up lines in the store because they are talking to the cashier about how their mother's third cousin's husband's best friend's wife just bought a pair of socks exactly like these ones and said they are the best things they ever purchased.

When you walk into the office of an I it is typical to see pictures of the person, the person's family, people they have met and interacted with, important people they have shaken hands with, pets, and so on. They like to get public recognition and proudly display awards and accomplishments.

Printed with permission from Lindsey Taylor

Depiction of an office of an I type individual. Note the focus on herself and her awards in the pictures on the walls.

Most I types are trendy dressers who like to have the latest clothing and hairstyles. They want to stand out, to be the center of attention. Being trendy helps cement this impression.

People who have I-type personalities are always extroverts with an upbeat, enthusiastic, inspirational, and emotional speaking style. They tend to be entertaining speakers who insert many personal stories and experiences into their speeches. They stay in touch with the audience, and they are always watching for the reactions of others. They are people-oriented, not task-oriented. Because of this, they talk more about themselves, about other people, and about team accomplishments than about tasks. They love being the center of attention.

I types like to talk. They would rather talk than listen. One time, I interviewed a guy for a business development role. He was a strong I personality. As it happened, it was an impromptu interview just prior to a previously scheduled meeting, and I only had twenty minutes with this individual. I had a number of questions to ask, so I needed to keep the answers to the point. However, I was only able to ask one question. The candidate took this question and talked for twenty minutes straight. I was unable to break into his dialogue – he just continued to talk. When the twenty minutes were up I stood, thanked him for coming, and ushered him out. He talked all the way through this. I made a decision right there not to hire him. No matter how good he said he was, if he could not listen to his "client," he was not fit for a business development role.

This was an extreme example. Most I types are not that intense. Typically, they are able to hear the emotional tones in other's voices, and they can respond or adjust accordingly. Although they can manage change well, they do not like high-risk, high-stress or high-conflict situations. This is perceived as negative, and it goes against the positive, upbeat nature of an I. They need a friendly work environment.

When implementing a project, I personalities prefer to work in teams. They do not like detailed work. They would prefer to network with and have others do the detailed tasks. They like input from other people before making a decision. When presenting an idea to them, it is best to show how this idea meets needs that they recognize. They are not great time managers and may need help with this. They typically ask "Who" questions.

"S" personalities

Someone with an S personality will bring whatever is required to a job interview. Depending on the circumstances, it might be a small portfolio or a large briefcase, but it will be well-organized and fit for the event. S types come to meetings with exactly what is required, logically thought out and neatly organized. Their objective in life is to help others perform consistently, to promote harmony, and to avoid conflict at all costs. They are consistent performers who prefer to work in predictable routines. They are practical and organized.

S personalities put some thought into whether they should travel light or bring bigger suitcases, and whether they should check their baggage or carry it on. The decision they make will be logically planned and well-organized. However, even after all their planning and organizing, they will check their bags if the attendant tells them that they should. This is to help promote harmony and avoid conflict. They will not rearrange the luggage in overhead bins to make room for their own luggage, but they will help others do this even if it means moving their own things to another location. They will never tell people what they think about the service, unless what they think is positive. In fact, to avoid any conflict caused by negative feedback, they might tell someone that the horrible service they just received was okay.

S types want to be liked. They are excellent team players, stable, patient, dependable, tolerant, logical, harmonious, and consistent. Under duress, however, they can become stubborn and hold a grudge.

When S personalities go shopping, they are always polite and thoughtful. In lineups at the cashier, they sometimes let others butt in front of them. They will give up their table in the food court for a family that seems to be stressed in finding a table. When shopping, they generally ensure that they are always following procedures. If they have sixteen items, they will not enter an express checkout line that has a limit of fifteen items. They don't like to haggle for items, as this is too stressful.

S people will have well-thought-out, organized resumes. They write clear and concise documentation, with complete information and excellent directions. They are great at conforming to predefined practices but not good at working in uncontrolled or undefined environments.

When you walk into the office of an S, you will typically see a well-organized environment. Everything will be filed neatly, with only work that is currently under way on the desktop. Pictures on the walls will be of the S and teams on which the S has worked or been involved.

Printed with permission from Lindsey Taylor

Depiction of an office of an S type individual. Note the focus on teams in the pictures on the walls.

It is hard to predict the way that S personalities will dress. Because they strive to be liked and popular, they will typically conform to the most popular dress styles within their environment, and they probably will not go to any extremes.

S personalities typically speak slowly and reflectively, centering their speech on practical issues. They like to lay things out in a logical, step-by-step procedure. They tend to be more introverted, but they are more people-focused than task-focused. As such, they will concentrate more on team accomplishments than on individual accomplishments. They do not like conflict and will do almost anything to avoid it. In stressful or high-conflict situations, they will have a tendency to become stubborn, and they will not negotiate.

On projects, S types like to take lead roles as long as the team is in harmony and working smoothly together. However, if asked or required, they can just as easily work as members of a team. S personalities are excellent listeners. They will really try to understand the speaker by listening for ways that they can help. They are patient and tolerant.

S types prefer to have things communicated to them in step-by-step, logical fashion, with lots of hands-on learning opportunities. Similarly, this is how they tend to communicate with others. S types prefer to deal with pre-established procedures and processes and perform consistently within stable, defined environments. They typically ask "How" questions.

"C" personalities

Someone with a C personality will typically bring a large briefcase or computer bag to a job interview. C personalities do not care about traveling light. Wherever they go they bring all kinds of things, because they never know when they might need an item. They will also bring their computer bag or briefcase to business meetings.

Because they are not light packers, when Cs travel they almost always check their luggage. They are usually quiet, preferring to endure inconveniences rather than to point things out in public and risk making a scene. However, they won't forget the inconvenience, whether it be poor service, a rude stewardess or waiter, or whatever. They won't hesitate to tell their acquaintances to avoid the company that caused them the inconvenience.

When Cs go shopping, like Ds they go prepared with a list. However, the Cs list is detailed with the precise features of each item they wish to purchase. In many cases, they will research their products beforehand, so that they understand exactly what they are purchasing. They will relentlessly compare features and prices, and from this, determine the best product in the market. You can pick Cs out in the store because they will be talking with a sales rep, asking all kinds of questions about the products. In many cases, the C will know more about the product than the sales rep. This, however, can upset the C. When that happens, he or she is likely to leave the store without making a purchase.

Cs will have complicated resumes that give all kinds of detail about past projects, education, and experience. I have conducted many interviews with high Cs and seen resumes that were literally a hundred pages long when you include project details, pictures, awards, recommendations, degrees, and reference letters provided for backup. I interviewed an applicant recently who showed up at my office with a stack of paper about two inches thick. That was his resume. It was amazing! It was thicker than some project specifications I've worked with.

Cs tend to spell everything out in great detail. Their work is logically ordered, precise, and mostly error-free. For example, we had a senior engineer who was a team lead for a number of individuals. As a team lead, he was responsible for completing yearly assessments for all of his team members. A typical yearly assessment is about six pages long. The assessments of this team lead were about twenty pages. He was forced by his manager to redo these assessments and reduce them to the proper six-page length.

When you walk into the office of a C you will typically see clutter. The offices of Cs are chock full of books, drawings, specifications, brochures, and charts, just to name a few things. Their walls are decorated with the same kinds of things. Sometimes this clutter extends outside their offices, where they wish to show important facts and details to anyone who walks past. No matter how messy or cluttered their offices, though, Cs always seem to know where everything is located.

Good example of an office of a C type individual. Note the clutter on the desk and on the walls.

Most Cs are not overly concerned with personal appearance. They can usually be identified by older, conservative styles. In many cases, they may appear to be quite dated, even disheveled. These people are known for their Einstein appearance, pocket protectors, and polyester suits.

C personality types are typically introverts. As such, they must be prompted and prodded to get a conversation started. They are careful not to show personal or emotional responses. However, once the C begins to build trust and rapport with an individual, the responses begin to get quite long and detailed. They also begin to ask questions back, to ensure that they have understood the original question and answered appropriately.

Cs like to work alone or as members of a small group. They do not like taking a lead role, as this places them in control of other people. This sort of responsibility just gets in their way and annoys them. Like D personalities, Cs are task-oriented, not people-oriented. They like to talk about their work, especially about how they were able to deliver on a project because of their innovations or efficient work practices. They love to demonstrate their expertise. They want to be sincerely recognized for legitimate accomplishments.

It takes a C a while to build trust and respect with others. If Cs are given incorrect data from someone, they tend to not trust that person anymore. Mistakes are not tolerated, and those who make mistakes are not to be trusted. As such, when presenting something to a C, ensure that your facts are straight and that you have presented the facts and figures in a sequential and logical fashion. Unlike Ds, who are strong in this area, Cs sometimes have difficulty creating mental pictures of an idea. It is best if you can present a visual interpretation of the idea, so the C can literally see what you are presenting.

Cs typically avoid high-risk, high-stress, and high-conflict situations. These types of environments are not productive for a C. Under these circumstances, they tend to recede back into a corner and keep to themselves. They typically ask "Why" questions.

How to apply this knowledge

When you have studied the personality profiles and are able to fairly accurately identify the profiles of people around you, the next step is the application of this knowledge to your interactions with other people. To maximize the effectiveness of each transaction, you need to determine your approach to dealing with people. Don't rely solely on your own personality strengths and weaknesses. Understand the strengths and weaknesses of each personality type and tailor your interactions to maximize the other person's strengths and minimize their weaknesses.

For example, after taking the DISC profile, I realized that I have a high D-C personality style. My DISC profile is a *Challenger*, which is the same name given to an Eight in the Enneagram profile system. I began to understand that I had to treat people with different profiles differently. For example:

- I had to have the patience to hear out the high Cs as they explained every aspect of the issue in great detail. I could not just bluntly ask them to get to the point. I had to take time for listening.

- I had to help the high S types cope with the enormous change they were seeing. I learned to realize that they could be overwhelmed by something I found so motivating.

- I had to learn to spend time talking to the I types about things other than work. I also had to ensure that they were not stuck in a back room in front of a computer all the time. When I phoned them, I had to start with some idle chitchat about the weekend before moving slowly into the reason for my call (unlike most Ds, who immediately want to get to the point). I couldn't start the conversation with a request.

- I had to ensure that the other Ds were given enough latitude to be independent, but not so much that the project suffered. That meant I had to transfer responsibility and decisions from me onto others.

- I also had to realize that with other Ds, I should not start conversations with idle chitchat. I tried this, but several D people told me to get to the point because they were busy and needed to get things done.

- I had to realize that we all like recognition, but each personality type requires different types of recognition at different frequencies.

- I had to communicate all of this to my team leads to ensure that they, too, were trying to optimize our corporate performance and relationships by dealing with people appropriately.

- I had to take time to communicate in person.

- I had to learn to communicate the same message to all people but using different techniques that engage each of the personality types.

Basically, in an effort to maximize my team's effectiveness, I began balancing my Personality Strength Zone with the Personality Strength Zone of my team members. This is the most important statement of this chapter. If you don't take anything else away from the personality profile section of this book, take this statement away:

The goal of personality profile training is to balance your Personality Strength Zone with the Personality Strength Zone of those you interact with, in an effort to maximize the efficiency and effectiveness of you and those around you.

Using DISC in dealing with people

The uses of the DISC system to enhance your people skills and to increase your effectiveness in real life are unlimited. The examples below illustrate how to use the DISC system in certain circumstances. There is no exact response for each circumstance, but as these examples illustrate, some general approaches may be taken.

 The following examples are available for download at www.StrengthZone.ca

Example One: A colleague, Jerry, is a high I. This colleague talks too loudly in the hallway outside your office, and when you are on the phone, it is distracting for you and the person to whom you are talking.

Possible Response: Engage Jerry in conversation about himself, his weekend, and his hobbies. Slowly lead into his work activities. Allow Jerry to talk about these activities for a few minutes. Do not cut him off or try to limit his responses. Sincerely complement Jerry on some of the work that he is involved in and his results, if appropriate. Mention that you know his role requires him to interact with others on a frequent basis and that you have noticed how others seem to enjoy talking with him. Then let Jerry know that his voice seems to carry very well, and that at times, it can be quite a distraction for you in your office. Ask Jerry if he can keep his voice lower or if he can move his conversations down the hall or into one of the nearby conference rooms.

Example Two: Take the same example, but now assume that Jerry is a high D.

Possible Response: Realize that Jerry is impatient and that you need to get to the point right away. Tell Jerry that his voice seems to carry well, and that when he is talking outside your office, it can be quite a distraction for you. Let him take some control by asking if there is a place he can take his hallway conversations that would be more private for both him and those around him.

Example Three: You need to ask Karen, a high S, to take on a task that she has never done before. You are sure she can do the task, based on her skills.

Possible Response: Knowing that high S people do not like sudden change or stress, approach Karen and carefully explain the situation. Describe the need for her to take on this task. Let Karen know that her involvement is greatly appreciated and that you will provide her with details about pre-established processes that have successfully been applied to this situation many times in the past. Let her know that you will check in with her periodically and that you are available should she have any questions or concerns.

Example Four: Fred, a high C, reports directly to you but spends too much time on what you consider to be insignificant detail, instead of on completing activities and showing some production.

Possible Response: Because high C people have a need to be organized and precise, you must explain logically and sincerely that you feel the detailed work he is doing is valuable and appreciated in some circumstances. Provide examples of how this detail is valuable, to show Fred that you are not just patronizing him. Then accurately describe the level of detail you would like Fred to work at. Provide precise examples of why it is important to work at this level, and show Fred how it benefits everyone, including him. Get a commitment from Fred to work at this level. Fully answer any questions Fred asks and indicate there are procedures for him to follow if he has additional concerns.

Example Five: In this example, I will provide the story. You need to determine the personality profile of the characters.

Fred has had a long, stressful week of meetings and contract negotiations in Houston and is boarding his flight home to Denver from the George W. Bush Intercontinental Airport. After being delayed for an hour due to mechanical difficulties, Fred pushes through the door of the airplane and heads for his seat. He sees Jane, the flight attendant, and just as she is about to welcome him and thank him for choosing Profile Airlines, he says, "I'm happy to see that your service is consistent – consistently late! I'm with XYZ Company, and thanks to your airline, I'm going to be late for my son's baseball game."

Fred shoots past her and proceeds to his seat, where people are already sitting. He opens the overhead bin only to find it already full of luggage. Meanwhile, Jane follows him down the isle, apologizing profusely for the delayed flight. "You should have seen the traffic in Denver this morning – I was lucky to make it to work before the flight left. It's a good thing the flight was delayed due to mechanical difficulties or I would have missed it. That wouldn't have looked very good, would it? A flight without a flight attendant! Turns out the mechanical problem was just a burned-out light bulb. We had a lousy ground crew when we landed in Houston. They wouldn't even clean the garbage out of the seat pockets. I had to do that myself, if you can believe it! But it's not a problem, because I am very versatile."

While Jane is talking, Fred moves suitcases around in the overhead bins, trying to get his carry-on bag to fit. George, sitting in the isle seat of the same row as Fred, finally stands up and says, "Hey, let me help you out. I can move my suitcase two rows back to the bin back there. That should leave enough room for your suitcase above our row."

Kate, in the window seat, notices that Fred has moved her suitcase to another bin. She doesn't say anything, but she makes a mental note about where her bag is and about the fact that Fred is rude and that he works for XYZ Company. One of her close friends is working on a project, and her friend had noted earlier that she was looking at adding XYZ Company to the bid list. Kate decides she will recommend to her friend that XYZ not be included.

- Jane has a _____ personality profile
- George has a _____personality profile
- Fred has a _____ personality profile
- Kate has a _____ personality profile

Example Six: In this example, I'll give you the same setting and characters, but this time changing the personality profiles.

Fred has had a long, stressful week of meetings and contract negotiations in Houston and is boarding his flight home to Denver from the George W. Bush Intercontinental Airport. After being delayed for an hour due to mechanical difficulties, Fred meanders through the door of the airplane and heads for his seat. He sees Jane, the flight attendant, and says to her, "Boy, am I happy that we are finally on our way home. I've had a hard week, and I'm really looking forward to sleeping in my own bed and seeing my family. Looks like I'll be late for my son's baseball game, but at least I'll make it. Do you know they made it to the state finals in their division this year?"

"I'm happy for you, sir," Jane responds. "Now please proceed to your seat. We have a full plane today, and I want to get everyone seated quickly."

Fred, a little taken back by Jane's response, dutifully moves past her and proceeds to his row, where people are already sitting. He reaches up and opens the overhead bin, only to find it already full of luggage.

Jane is dispensing with the other passengers in a very businesslike manner, getting them seated and settled as quickly as possible. While Fred is trying to get his suitcase to fit, he tries to strike up a conversation with George, who is sitting in the isle seat deeply engrossed in the book he is reading. "So, are you on your way home to Denver?" asks Fred.

George looks up and replies, "No."

"So you must be transferring from Denver to another location?" Fred responds with an encouraging smile.

George, already back in his book, looks up again. "No."

Fred, still trying to stow his suitcase, has not noticed that George is reading and replies "Oh. So why are you going to Denver?"

This time with an annoyed look on his face, George says, "I'm going for a conference on the application of fast Fourier transforms to digital signal processing in the area of MRI imaging."

Just then Jane taps Fred on the shoulder and says, "Excuse me sir, if you cannot find a place for your luggage you will have to check it."

By this time, Kate, in the window seat, has noticed the trouble that Fred is having. She pipes up, saying, "Excuse me, but there is an empty bin two rows up that your suitcase could fit in."

"Those overhead bins are reserved for the passengers in business class only," Jane immediately replies.

Kate, a little embarrassed by Jane's abrupt response, stammers, "I'm sorry. I was only trying to help. I have some room under my seat. Maybe your suitcase will fit under there. I don't mind."

Fred cheerfully hands his suitcase to Jane. "No problem. I'll check my bag. I know I'll be late for my son's baseball game anyway, so I guess a few more minutes won't hurt." He settles into the middle seat between George and Kate, saying, "Did you know that my son's baseball team made it to the state finals this year? They've done very well, considering that their coach is just a college kid. Yep, a college kid taking a psychology major."

- Jane has a _____ personality profile
- George has a _____ personality profile
- Fred has a _____ personality profile
- Kate has a _____ personality profile

 Application exercise

1. Create a response to Example One on page 122 assuming that Jack is a high C. Create another response assuming Jack is a high S.

2. Create responses to examples Three and Four on pages 122 and 123 for the remaining personality types for Karen and Fred.

3. Take the check sheets provided at the end of this chapter to your next meeting or interview or when you are traveling. Use them to determine the DISC attribute of at least one person in the meeting or interview. Do this each day for a week. List the results below. Try to meet with that person in a different setting the following week to verify your assessment. If possible, have that person take the actual DISC profile and compare results.

	Person's Name	DISC Analysis #1	DISC Analysis #2
1			
2			
3			
4			
5			

 Check sheets
The following check sheets are available for download at www.StrengthZone.ca

Visual Clues

D	Brings only a notebook or small portfolio to an interview or meeting
D	Does not bring anything to the interview or meeting
D	Travels with carry-on baggage only whenever possible
D	Adjusts luggage in the overhead bins on aircraft to make room for their own luggage above or close to their own seat
D	Stands up to adversity
D	Bold, risk-taker
D	Determined shopper
D	Written communication is precise and to the point
D	Well-organized office environment, somewhat stark
D	Conservative dress and styles
I	Doesn't spend a lot of time taking notes in meetings – prefers to talk
I	Meets new people all the time – talks with strangers
I	Loves to shop and browse leisurely with friends – strikes up conversations with cashier
I	Tend to work with others to get written communication complete
I	Office environment has pictures of family, friends, pets, acquaintances
I	Stylishly dressed with latest clothing and hairstyles
S	Comes to a meeting well-organized with proper materials
S	Logical approach to everything
S	Consistent performers and predictable routines
S	Looks for ways to promote harmony in situations around them and will go out of the way to avoid conflict
S	May help people rearrange luggage in overhead bins even if it means inconveniencing themselves
S	Doesn't provide negative feedback, even with poor service
S	Clear, concise written communication
S	Prefers teamwork
S	Office is typically neat, organized with self-portraits and pictures of teams
C	Brings a large briefcase or computer bag to an interview or meeting
C	Detailed resumes
C	Detailed reports that are well-organized, logically presented, precise and virtually error-free.
C	While shopping for an item will spend a lot of time asking the sales reps detailed questions about products
C	Written communication includes all kinds of details
C	Office is cluttered with all kind of detail
C	Conservative to disheveled styles

Verbal Clues

	D	Direct, to the point
	D	Commanding speakers focusing on their own objectives
	D	Talks about activities and results rather than people
	D	Frustrated by lack of action
	D	Likes to have lead roles
	D	Asks people to get to the point
	D	Poor listeners
	D	Can work well in high-stress, high-risk, and high-conflict situations
	D	Deals with concepts, not details
	D	Asks "what" type questions
	D	Prefers to communicate with metaphors or analogies
	I	Upbeat, enthusiastic, inspirational, and emotional speaking style
	I	Entertaining speakers relating many personal stories and experiences
	I	Watches for the reaction of others
	I	People-oriented, not task-oriented
	I	Loves being the center of attention
	I	Would rather talk than listen
	I	Can hear the emotional tones in other's voices
	I	Doesn't like high-stress, high-risk, or high-conflict situations
	I	Prefers working in a team and getting input from others before making a decision
	I	Asks "who" type questions
	S	Speaks slowly and reflectively
	S	Speech is centered around practical issues
	S	Lays things out in logical, step-by-step procedures
	S	Team-focused rather than task-focused
	S	Avoids conflict and promotes harmony
	S	Excellent listeners, always trying to find ways to help in situations
	S	Typically ask "how" type questions
	C	Must be prompted and prodded to get a conversation started
	C	Doesn't show emotional responses
	C	Once a level of trust is established, provides detailed answers to questions
	C	Likes to work alone or in a small group
	C	Doesn't like lead roles
	C	Talks about work and how they delivered on a project, not about people
	C	Loves to demonstrate and talk about their work
	C	Mistakes are not acceptable
	C	Can best understand a concept by providing a visual interpretation
	C	Avoids high-risk, high-stress, and high-conflict situations
	C	Asks "why" questions

Talents

· 5 ·

Since the greatest room for each person's growth is in the areas of his greatest strength, you should focus your training time and money on educating him about his strengths and figuring out ways to build on these strengths rather than on remedially trying to plug his skill gaps.

> - Now, Discover Your Strengths by
> Marcus Buckingham and Donald Clifton

Whatever you set your mind to, you will be most successful when you craft your role to play to your signature talents most of the time.

> - Now, Discover Your Strengths by
> Marcus Buckingham and Donald Clifton

A definition of talents, skills, and knowledge

The third step in defining your Strength Zone is to understand your dominant talents – your Talent Strength Zone. Your greatest personal growth will occur when you are operating in your areas of greatest strength. You can become much more efficient in any role if you concentrate on your areas of strength and work to improve in these areas. Jim Sundberg summarized this when he stated, "Discover your uniqueness; then discipline yourself to develop it." This chapter and its exercises will help you identify your greatest talents, which I call your Talent Strength Zone. Then it will be up to you to discipline yourself to develop these talents or your uniqueness.

There is a distinct difference between talents, skills, and knowledge. Here are the *Webster's Dictionary* definitions:

- **Talent** – a special natural ability.

- **Skill** – the ability to do something well. Expertness or dexterity in performance.

- **Knowledge** – familiarity, understanding or information gained by study or experience.

In their book, *First, Break All the Rules*, Marcus Buckingham and Curt Coffman categorize talents, skills, and knowledge as follows:

- **Talent** – A naturally recurring pattern of thought, feeling or behavior.

- **Skill** – Steps of an activity.

- **Knowledge** – Facts and lessons learned. Factual and experiential.

According to this definition, a talent is a thought, feeling, or behavior that occurs or recurs naturally. Some examples of talent are singers with perfect pitch, musicians who play by ear without sheet music, the speed of a sprinter, or the grace and finesse of a ballet dancer. These are all talents, although the talents that we concentrate on here are not focused on the physical as much as they are focused on the cerebral.

Just because you have a talent in a particular area doesn't mean that you don't have to work at this talent to fully develop. It just means that you find this area easiest to work in (and probably more enjoyable) than other areas.

A good example of raw talent is Michael Jordan. Perhaps the best athlete to ever live, Jordan's raw talent far surpassed the developed talent of many National Basketball Association players. However, the thing that made Michael Jordan really stand out was that he recognized his strengths and worked hard to develop them – to the point that on the court, he became an almost unstoppable force. Each week, he spent many hours developing his skills in the area of his talent. He would practice shooting, dunking, passing, and dribbling for hours, even after practice when the rest of the team had left.

In contrast, Mickey Mantle – one of the best baseball players of all time – greatly limited his effectiveness by not capitalizing on his talents. Mantle was well-known for his drinking binges and his aversion to practice in the off-season. Most baseball experts agree that Mantle never achieved his full potential. He was expected to surpass players like Joe DiMaggio and Babe Ruth. It never happened because Mantle did not develop his talents. He relied on his raw talent and a minimal amount of practice. In doing this, he limited his potential.

The key to success is to identify your talents and then build on these talents by developing skills and gaining knowledge. You can use skills and knowledge to improve in an area of strength (or weakness), but skills are not talents, nor can knowledge about a subject be called a talent. Anyone can gain knowledge or acquire skills in any area, regardless of their natural talents, but no one can become talented in a particular area unless raw, undeveloped talent is already present. Later in this chapter, we will discuss this idea further. In the next chapter, we will discuss in more detail how to develop skills and knowledge in your strength areas.

John C. Maxwell has stated (my paraphrase) that people will not pay for average. People only want to pay for good to excellent. If skill is rated on a scale of one to ten, with one being the lowest, people will not pay for anything under a score of six – and, realistically, they want to see a score of eight or higher. Maxwell goes further by stating that if you are sitting at a skill level of one in some area, there is no use trying to raise this to an eight because most people can only raise their score in a particular area by one or two points. This rise in score does not come easily, either. It can be compared to the 80/20 rule. Your current level was probably arrived at with twenty percent effort. To go from where you are now to a few points higher will require approximately four times this effort. It will be even more difficult if you are not talented in the area in which you are trying to improve. Therefore, you need to understand what you are talented at and build on these attributes, rather than waste time on things that will not provide value. This is your Talent Strength Zone.

I saw a great example of this in the difference between our business development group and our engineering group on Lilongwe. For the most part, these two groups of people came from engineering backgrounds (mostly electrical, control, or instrumentation) and all were of above-average intelligence.

On Lilongwe, they all started out working on projects in an engineering office and followed this work up with time spent at the client's site implementing their design.

Members of the engineering group were really good at being analytical. They liked searching for (and finding) the optimal solution. They liked evaluating risks before acting. They thrived in this environment. In some cases, they even thought the client was just a nuisance who had to be dealt with before completing their work. Connecting with and relating to the client did not energize them; it was just something that had to be done.

Although members of the business development group were good at the technical work, they were not energized by it. As time went on, the business development engineers began to realize that they were really good at connecting with people, at relating to people, and at meeting new people. They seemed to thrive in an environment that allowed them to do this.

Eventually, the business development engineers began to move into positions that allowed them to work in their relationship talent zone, and the "techie" engineers stayed in positions that allowed them to remain technical. Although, we didn't know it at the time, the members of these two groups were beginning to identify their areas of unique talent, and were starting to develop their skills and knowledge in these areas.

Talent theory

Marcus Buckingham and Donald O. Clifton in their book *Now, Discover Your Strengths* state that once developed, primary talents cannot be changed. You may learn new skills or acquire new knowledge in a talent area, but you cannot create new talents. This theory is based on knowledge about the development of the human brain and on our current understanding of this development process. Essentially, your talents are determined biologically by about 15 years of age, and these talents will not change over time.

Talent development

The cells in your brain, called neurons, communicate with each other using a connection called a synapse. This connection between the cells in your brain determines your behavior, and therefore, your talents.

A human being is born with 100 billion neurons. Shortly before birth, the infant's brain cells begin to form these connections. The synapses continue to form until the child is between ages three and five. During this time, each neuron forms approximately 15,000 connections, resulting in 100 billion times 15,000 connections. This network is incredibly intricate and unique for each person.

After you reach age five, the synapse connection process stops. Many of the synapses that were created during this time of rapid brain growth are no longer used, falling into disrepair and gradually breaking. By the time you are sixteen, only half of the connections you had at age five still exist.

New synapses can be created at any age (as can be seen in those people who need to learn new skills due to injuries) but the majority of your mental network does not change after you reach your mid-teens.

This is articulated in a publication entitled *The Growth of Your Amazing Neural Network*, found at The Franklin Institute Online (www.fi.edu/brain). Here's an extract:

> *Before birth you created neurons, the brain cells that communicate with each other, at the rate of 15 million per hour! When you emerged into the world, your 100 billion neurons were primed to organize themselves in response to your new environment – no matter the culture, climate, language, or lifestyle.*
>
> *During infancy, billions of these extraordinary cells intertwined into the vast networks that integrated your nervous system. By the time you were four or five years old, your fundamental cerebral architecture was complete.*
>
> *Until your early teens, various windows of opportunity opened when you could*

most easily learn language and writing, math and music, as well as the coordinated movements used in sports and dance. But, at any age you can – and should – continue to build your brain and expand your mind.

This is the basis of Buckingham and Clifton's book. They state that a person's genetics and environment causes the brain to use some synapses more than others. These synapses are used so much that they become able to carry much more traffic, and they are much more efficient than other synapses. In effect, they become like superhighways or T1 communication links. Conversely, some synapses rarely get used. These synapses wither away and become unusable.

Stated another way, a synapse that is not used often is like a dial-up Internet connection versus the hundred-megabit-per-second Internet connection for a synapse that is used a lot. Now, there are times when the dial-up connection is still needed, but it is hugely inefficient compared to the hundred-megabit-per-second connection that we have in our offices. Taking this analogy just a little farther, in the engineering world, it is quite common to have to travel to a third-world nation that does not have high-speed Internet. Downloads of data or even simple email can be frustrating and inefficient.

In my experience on Lilongwe, this is similar to placing an engineer who is used to working on projects by himself in a business development role. The technical engineer may be able to function in a business development capacity, but he will definitely not be using a hundred-megabit-per-second connection.

Buckingham and Clifton go on to define these data superhighway synapses, or T1 communication links, as talents. If you love to learn about all kinds of things, you may have a learning talent, a learning superhighway. If you cannot seem to understand people and their feelings, you may not have an empathy talent.

Moreover, Buckingham and Clifton go on to say that if you do not have a talent in a particular area, you cannot acquire that talent. You can become aware of the weakness in that area, and you can gain knowledge and even skills to compensate, but that area will never be a dominant talent or strength. It will never be a superhighway, a T1 communication synapse.

Over the years, I have observed a number of people promoted to a role for which they were qualified and watched them operate adequately in this role. However, in some cases, these people became unhappy, even bitter, because the role required the use of talents they did not have. They were unable to adapt the role to the talents that they did have. In some cases, this bitterness led to disciplinary action, resignation, and layoffs. A little later in this chapter, we will discuss redefining your role to fit your talents.

Identifying your talents

The process of trying to define your strengths identifying your T1 superhighways – your talents – is critical. In his book *The Effective Executive* Peter Drucker says it was crucial for people to make their strengths productive, and the only way to do this was for them to first identify their strengths. Drucker provided a few questions for readers to answer. Summarized below, these questions start to point readers in the direction of what their strengths may be.

 The following questions are available for download at www.StrengthZone.ca:

Am I a listener or a reader?
- Do I prefer to be briefed on subjects verbally?
- Does this need to be followed up by a written summary?
- Do I prefer to have a written or verbal report to summarize issues?

How do I learn?
- Do I take notes while listening?
- Do I prefer to read and take notes?
- Do I prefer to listen and not take notes?
- Do I prefer to talk, to summarize my learning verbally?

General questions:
- Do I work well with people?
- In what relationship do I work well with people: leader, follower, team lead, team member, mentor, coach (list all that apply)?
- What time of day do I work best?
- Do I perform well under stress?
- Do I need a highly structured environment?

- Do I work best as a minnow in a large organization or as a large fish in a small organization?
- Do I produce results as a decision maker or an advisor?
- Am I able to think through reports and make the tough decisions (am I a decision-maker who takes command responsibility, rather than a staff thinker who organizes and lays out problems)?
- Am I a good negotiator?
- What am I good at negotiating?

How do I write?
- Do I need many drafts?
- Do I work meticulously on each sentence until it is correct?
- Do I need a document outline before I start?
- Do I work best by marking up an existing document (to build on it) or by creating one (am I a mechanic or a designer)?
- Am I effective at writing up the final report?

How do I speak in public?
- Do I require prepared text?
- Do I require rough notes?
- Do I speak from memory?
- Do I not like public speaking at all?
- Do I prefer to use PowerPoint or no visual presentation?

This is an excellent exercise. To help ensure that you are working in the most efficient method possible, make sure you take the time to answer these questions. But answering these questions does not help in identifying your dominant talents. The only source I have found that does this is Buckingham and Clifton's book, *Now, Discover Your Strengths*.

Talent themes

According to Buckingham and Clifton, you have only five dominant synapses or talents. You may have other secondary talents, but they aren't nearly as strong as your five dominant talents.

Buckingham and Clifton define a total of thirty-four talent themes. These are briefly summarized below. Refer to their book for the detailed descriptions.

1. **Achiever:** This talent is illustrated in a quote taken from *The Fred Factor:* "Look to every day as a new day, and make each day better than the last. Even on my days off, I have goals, and I feel like I need to get a lot done. If I feel like I wasted the day, I don't sleep quite as well at night."
2. **Activator:** Impatient for action – only action leads to performance.
3. **Adaptability:** Live for the moment. Able to respond to the demands of the moment and change plans as required.
4. **Analytical:** Objective and dispassionate. Theories must be backed with facts.
5. **Arranger:** Likes taking complex, multivariable situations and aligning all the variables until the optimal solution is reached.
6. **Belief:** Enduring core values. Typically family-oriented with high ethics. Altruistic. Values responsibility.
7. **Command:** Likes to take charge of situations. Has no problem in doing so and in letting people know how things really are.
8. **Communication:** Energized by public speaking and writing in a way that energizes other people.
9. **Competition:** Very aware of the performance of others and must outperform others.
10. **Connectedness:** Considerate, caring, and accepting. Bridge builder. Believes that all people are connected.
11. **Context:** Looking back to the past to find answers for the present. The past provides knowledge of how things should be handled now.
12. **Deliberative:** Careful and cautious. Evaluates risks before acting.
13. **Developer:** Sees potential in others and wants to help them develop it.
14. **Discipline:** Needs things to be structured and predictable, ordered and planned.
15. **Empathy:** Senses the emotions of others. Has the ability to see through the eyes of others.
16. **Fairness:** Balance is important. Needs to treat everyone the same way.
17. **Focus:** Needs a clear destination. Goal-setting is important.
18. **Futuristic:** Is able to perceive or paint the future and loves trying to do this.
19. **Harmony:** Helps others find areas for agreement. Is adverse to

conflict. Finds common ground between contentious issues.

20. **Ideation:** Fascinated with new concepts, with familiar challenges, or with new and disparate phenomena.
21. **Inclusiveness:** Needs to include people, not exclude them. Is distressed by seeing people on the outside looking in.
22. **Individualization:** Able to observe and identify uniqueness in every individual. Able to identify and pull out strengths in all people.
23. **Input:** Inquisitive. A collector.
24. **Intellection:** Likes to think. Likes mental activities. Likes to develop ideas or solve problems.
25. **Learner:** Loves learning. The process of learning, as opposed to the subject matter, is important.
26. **Maximizer:** Taking something strong to something superb, as opposed to moving from substandard to above average. Excellenceis the measure.
27. **Positivity:** Generous with praise and quick to smile. Lighthearted optimist.
28. **Relator:** Is pulled toward familiar people. Is not necessarily shy in front of strangers, but gets a great deal of pleasure from close friends.
29. **Responsibility:** Takes ownership for anything that is committed to. Follows through to completion.
30. **Restorative:** Loves to solve problems. Enjoys analyzing symptoms and finding a solution.
31. **Self-assurance:** Self-confidence. Has faith in own strengths and in own judgment.
32. **Significance:** Needs to be recognized for accomplishments. Wants to push others to achievement and recognition.
33. **Strategic:** Able to navigate though obstacles and to chart the best route between two points.
34. **Woo** (Winning Others Over): Enjoys the challenge of meeting new people and getting them to like you.

As mentioned previously, everyone has five main themes. With thirty-four different themes, there are more than thirty-three million combinations of the top five themes, which means the chance that you are exactly the same as someone else is quite slim. Also, each one of your themes does not stand on its own. Rather, it is uniquely interwoven with your other themes, so that even if someone did have the same top five themes, that person would probably be quite different from you.

This unique combination of talents is your Talent Strength Zone.

Talent examples

Now let's look at examples of talents in the individuals I worked with on the Lilongwe project, as well as on some other, more recent projects. For a list of examples of all thirty-four talents, refer to Chapter Four of *Now, Discover Your Strengths*.

Achiever: The person who comes immediately to mind for the Lilongwe project is me. I have to have a system in place to measure my progress against preset goals. I have to make progress against these goals. My goals are balanced between personal, relationships, health, career, fun, and financial. I have to measure progress in each of these areas each week and review these goals daily. It is not good enough to achieve one thing per month. I have to achieve something daily. This does not have to be a major accomplishment, but it does have to be something that takes me a step closer toward a major accomplishment. Making progress yesterday is not good enough. I need to accomplish something each and every day.

Analytical: One of our project managers has this talent. He loves to look at different project scenarios and calculate what the gross profit would be in each scenario. This is a fairly complex calculation, including such things as rebates received, commissions paid, employee margins on straight time, employee margins on overtime, employee margins with uplifted salaries, and margins on contractors. He also spends time looking at patterns within the portion of the project that has already been executed. He comes up with conclusions based on his research and uses these conclusions to tweak his project and make it better.

Significance: Another one of our project managers has this talent. He is excellent at managing projects, but he does expect to stand out. He wants people to notice him and the work he is doing. If the project he is working on does not allow him to stand out, he may use circumstances in his personal life to get attention.

Learner: A number of people I have worked with on projects have had this talent. These people are always striving to learn something new. It does not have to be work-related, and it may be totally different from what you might expect from that person. Other individuals with this talent seem to focus on a particular area; they are quite interested in becoming experts in this particular area.

Intellection: We had a technical lead on the Lilongwe project who had this talent. He liked to get away by himself and think through issues and problems. He did not like to make snap decisions, and he did not like to be interrupted while he was alone thinking. He was the first person in our company to make it known that he was not to be disturbed between 1 and 2 pm each day. This had been unheard of in our company before this time, as we prided ourselves on an open-door policy. Since this individual started his practice, however, others have seen the benefit and built reflection time into their own schedules.

Talent research and tools

Note that the discussion on talents so far has concentrated on the work done by Clifton and Buckingham. This is primarily because the work they have done is outstanding. I have not found anything else that even comes close. This is after spending countless hours reading, searching the Internet, and doing research. Clifton and Buckingham, in conjunction with the Gallop organization, have conducted two million interviews in the process of perfecting their talent profile tool. Thus, it is based not only on scientific study, but also on statistical evaluation not available to many other researchers or authors outside the Gallop organization.

Their talent profile tool is available on their website, www.strengthsfinder.com but cannot be accessed without a code that you get when you purchase their book, *Now, Discover Your Strengths*. We'll talk more about this later. A link to their website is also available from www.StrengthZone.ca.

Perfect talent combination

There is no such thing as a perfect (or best) talent combination. Few people in this world have matching talents. Even if the five primary talents are the same for two people, the combination of how their talents are interwoven, and how each person has developed these talents, will be unique. Conversely, examples abound of people who have unique talent combinations but work in essentially the same types of jobs and who are extremely effective in this role. Take the U.S. presidency, for example. Ronald Reagan and George W. Bush were both effective enough to be elected for second terms, but these two presidents possessed vastly different talents.

On the Lilongwe project, one of our technical leads had the following talents: *Intellection, Consistency, Learner, Developer,* and *Inquisitive*. Another one of our technical leads had these talents: *Consistency, Focus, Competition, Harmony,* and *Deliberative*. These are quite different talents, yet these individuals each performed extremely well in the role of technical lead.

Within our business unit, one of our project managers had the following talents: *Ideation, Significance, Futuristic, Intellection,* and *Analytical*. These are quite different from my talents, *Maximizer, Achiever, Ideation, Learner,* and *Belief*, yet we were both able to manage and complete successful projects.

Having said this, certain talents lend themselves to certain professions (note that I said talents, and not talent combinations). For example, someone in a sales role, who needs to cold call prospective clients, would probably benefit greatly from the *Woo* talent. Similarly, a family counselor would probable benefit from the *Empathy* talent; a DNA scientist would benefit from the *Intellection* talent; an account manager would benefit from the *Relator* talent; and an emergency room trauma physician would undoubtedly benefit from the *Command* talent, just to name a few.

In any role, success depends on how well you understand your talents and how well you adapt your role to take advantage of these talents.

Why is knowing your dominant talents important?

Knowing your dominant talents is extremely important to your success as an individual, mostly because these are the areas in which you operate most naturally and efficiently. These dominant talents represent the areas where you can make the biggest gains with the least pain. Trying to develop in the areas of your lesser talents may buy you some success, but you will never experience the same success as when you begin to develop in the areas of your Talent Strength Zone. Trying to develop in other talent areas will also cause a lot of frustration.

Let's go back to John C. Maxwell's statement that people will not pay for average. People only want to pay for good to excellent. If skill is rated on a scale of one to ten, with one being the lowest, people will not pay for anything under a score of six, and realistically, people want to see a score of eight or higher. Maxwell goes further by stating that if you have a skill level of one in some area, there is no use trying to raise this to an eight because most people can only raise their score in any particular area by one or two points. This rise in score does not come easily, either. It can be compared to the 80/20 rule. Your current level was probably arrived at with twenty percent of the effort. To go from where you are now to even a few points higher will require approximately four times the effort. This will be even more difficult if you are not talented in the area in which you are trying to improve. Therefore, you need to understand what you are talented at and build on these attributes, rather than waste time on things that will not provide value.

The Gallup organization did related research on the satisfaction of people in the workplace, and the results were captured in *First, Break all the Rules* by Marcus Buckingham and Curt Coffman. For this project, Gallup asked 1.7 million people in 101 companies around the world a number of workplace-related questions. One of these questions was, "Do you have the opportunity to do what you do best in your workplace?" The astounding result was that only twenty percent of respondents felt that they were working in the area of their strengths. This means that eighty percent of the global workforce is working inefficiently. Other studies have shown that the results of this inefficiency are:

- Higher turnover
- Higher sick rate
- Stress on the job
- Sickness caused by stress on the job
- Low productivity

This list could go on and on, but the point is that the result of people not knowing about their strengths and not working in their strength areas has huge costs personally, socially, and financially.

Conversely, people who are able to identity their talents and find ways to work within their talents have a huge advantage. Let's go back to the Braveheart example. Recall that William Wallace's use of values united his troops into a fighting machine and won the Scots their freedom against the British. But what about his talents?

Wallace was obviously talented with a sword and with other weapons of war, but what about his other talents? I believe that Wallace was an effective catalyst for the Scots because he recognized his own talents and was able to work within his Talent Strength Zone. In the movie, he displayed the following talents:

- Command: He was able to take charge of situations both on and off the battlefield. In the movie, these situations were recorded as he progressed through his life, first as a young man and then as the leader of the Scottish forces against the English.

- Strategic: He was able to navigate through all of the obstacles placed before him. These obstacles were on a personal level as well as on a military level. He was extremely strategic on the battlefield, and he routinely outsmarted the English off the battlefield as well.

- Belief: He definitely displayed core values. As outlined earlier, the enduring core value for himself and for his people was freedom.

- Communication: Wallace seemed energized by public speaking. Whether he spoke to his own people and troops or in defiance of the English, his speeches were well received and highly motivating for his people.

What is the goal of the test?

The initial goal of the talent test is simply to identify your dominant talents – your Talent Strength Zone.

The goal of the personality profile is to identify your personality strengths and weaknesses and to understand how these strengths and weaknesses affect you in your daily communication with others. Once you understand this, you can try to adjust your style to ensure that you are communicating effectively with everyone. In effect, the goal is to capitalize on your own Personality Strength Zone while maximizing the Personality Strength Zone of those around you.

This is somewhat different than the initial goal for the talent test, which is to concentrate on building your talent strengths and working in your Talent Strength Zone, not worrying much about your talent weaknesses. Once you have identified your talents and adjusted your own role to take advantage of your talents, however, the next step is to help others through the same process. You will be more effective if you can identify talents that others have and assist them in redefining their roles to take full advantage of their talents. Even better when you are able to move others – who are strong in talent areas that you lack – into roles that complement your own. Whether you are in an official position of leadership or not, helping those around you become better people will help you as well.

Elbert Hubbard has stated, "There is something that is much more scarce, something finer by far, something rarer than ability. It is the ability to recognize ability."

The ability to recognize ability, however, has to be taken a step further. Not only do you need to be able to recognize ability, you need to be able to help the person with ability focus on that ability and structure his or her roles around this ability in a way that maximizes effectiveness. So Hubbard's quote could be rewritten as, "There is something much more scarce, something finer by far, something rarer than ability. It is the ability to recognize ability and to develop this ability to its ultimate potential.

Having stated this, one would think that recognizing ability simply adds to the effectiveness of people, but I suggest that it actually multiplies their effectiveness.

I liken this to a pyramid scheme, except that it is beneficial to everyone, including those on the bottom, and it is not illegal. What I mean by this is that if you help others find their Strength Zone and show them how to work within their zones, both you and the other person will become more effective. This is an additive effect.

However, if you also show these people how to recognize ability and how to teach these concepts to others, then they go off and do this, you have quickly created a pyramid that is self-building, one that will continue to build infinitely. This is a multiplication effect (as shown in the following diagram).

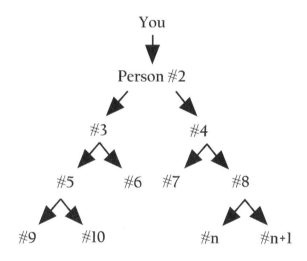

Thus the ultimate goal of the talent test is to identify your talents, to begin to work within these talents, and to help others do the same so that you are always building an expanding network of people working within their Talent Strength Zone.

Take the test

You can identify your five main talents by taking the online evaluation located at www.strengthsfinder.com. The Clifton StrengthsFinder is the first assessment instrument of this type developed expressly for the Internet. However, before you can take this evaluation, you must purchase the book (or CD-ROM) *Now, Discover Your Strengths*. It can be found at any major bookstore or Internet bookstore. Inside is a unique code. Entering this code on the website gains you access to the test, which is comprised of 180 questions. You are limited to twenty seconds per question for a total of thirty to forty minutes for the entire test. This speed-test approach is designed to bring out your first – and strongest – reaction to each question. If the instrument allowed more time for answers, users would have more time to try to apply logic, and the test would become less effective. The StrengthsFinder site can also be accessed by clicking on the link provided at www.StrengthZone.ca.

I believe this is a valuable evaluation tool and that everyone should take this test. If you are not able to purchase the book, the next best thing would be to ask your close friends and business associates to look at the thirty-four talents listed earlier in this chapter and select what they feel are your top five talents. I would ask for between five and ten opinions. From this, you should be able to determine your overall top five talents. This will be a good start at trying to identify your talents, but it will not be nearly as accurate as the test itself. For this purpose, an evaluation sheet is provided at the end of the chapter, as well as in downloadable form at www.StrengthZone.ca.

Your results

When you have completed the test, your results will immediately be displayed online as a list of your top five of the thirty-four talents with a description of each. This is your Talent Strength Zone.

The first question you will probably ask is, "What does it mean?" or "What can I do with this?"

First, these primary talents may not yet be areas of strength for you. The test did not anoint you with talents or with strengths. As described earlier, your talents are a combination of genetics and environment developed over the first fifteen years of your life. But this does not mean that you have learned how to take advantage of them. The first thing you should do after identifying your primary talents is to read and ponder the descriptions. Take some reflective time to further understand your unique talent combination. *Now, Discover Your Strengths* has excellent descriptions and examples of each of the talents. These examples take the form of excerpts from the lives of people working in typical careers. I found them to be quite informative.

According to Buckingham and Clifton, the test is accurate approximately 80 percent of the time (varies between .785 and .8 as per explanation on page 252 of "Now, Discover Your Strengths"). As well, the results will not change significantly over time or if you take the test multiple times. Once you understand these results, your task is to build your talents into strengths. This will be discussed further in the following chapters, but it involves one or more of the following:

1. Adapt your current role to take advantage of your talents

2. Move out of your current role into one that allows you to capitalize on your talents if you have reviewed your current role and there is no way that you can use your talents to enhance that role.

3. Build on your talents by building your knowledge and skills in your talent areas

As an example, a person who has the *Woo* talent but works in an office cubicle and has little interaction with others may want to find another role. If you have the *Woo* talent, you enjoy the challenge of meeting new people and getting them to like you. Working in an isolated office environment is not a good application of this talent. Many opportunities exist in the workplace for people with the *Woo* talent: management, sales, customer service, and public relations are good examples. The important thing to remember is that people with this talent are good at meeting and forming relationships with others.

If one of your talents is *Maximizer* (which just happens to be one of mine), and you are working in a role that requires you to take projects or products that are in trouble and turn them around, you may want to look for another role. People who have the *Maximizer* talent do well at transforming something strong into something superb, which takes just as much effort, but is much more thrilling for them than taking something from below average to just above average. As another example, a person who has the *Maximizer* talent could flourish in a role requiring the building of a superb new product by incorporating the best features of a number of other successful products.

When I write engineering design documents, or when I am writing responses to requests for proposals on potential projects, I am lost when I have to create documents from scratch. I always, without exception, look to see what similar documents have already been written. I then take the relevant pieces from these documents and build my documents. This is another good example of my *Maximizer* talent at work.

Conversely, writing this book was an extreme challenge for me. Because there is nothing else like it on the market, I had nothing to start with. Just a blank piece of paper.

This is in complete contrast to one of the engineers who worked with me for more than fifteen years. One of his talents was *Intellection*, defined as someone who likes to develop ideas or solve problems. He was not interested in using the work of others as a baseline. He always wanted to start his documents from scratch. For him, starting with an existing document resulted in inefficiencies. In some cases, he was almost paralyzed when forced to start with someone else's document as a baseline.

Nothing is fundamentally incorrect with either approach. The problem of lost efficiencies arises when you do not take the time to determine how you function most efficiently. Only when you know this can you begin to work at peak effectiveness. Peter Drucker says that everyone must strive to work in their strength areas. The StrengthsFinder tool helps you define your talents. You must then determine how best to take advantage of these talents.

We see the ability to recognize a talent and to build it into a towering strength in most major corporations in North America. The corporations have a management structure with a chief executive officer (CEO), chief financial officer (CFO), chief operating officer (COO), and human resource officer (HRO) at the top. From there, the company may decide to add more positions at the top level and to begin subdividing responsibilities into presidents and vice presidents of divisions.

The point I want to make here is that the people chosen for these top positions are often not interchangeable. Besides the obvious differences in skills, people at this level have come to recognize, to some extent, their personal talents. They have been able to take advantage of these talents to help them define appropriate performance and behavior for their current role. This has allowed them to work within a strength zone that they have defined specifically for this role. The definition may not be formal, but it is quite distinctive.

For example, a COO personality is typically meticulous at managing existing processes, while the CEO needs to be a leader with vision, a person who can see beyond and through existing processes to the outside world and who can continuously adapt the organization and its processes to match or stay in front of the marketplace and keep the organization viable.

This is not to say that someone in a COO role can never move into a CEO role, but it would take a huge paradigm shift on the part of the COO. The COO would have to re-evaluate his talents and learn how to redefine himself and his responses to situations by applying his talents differently. Instead of fastidiously managing pre-existing processes with little or no change, the COO/CEO would have to move to the other end of the spectrum and begin to challenge any archaic processes that are costing the company potential market share. They would have to be able to see the true market outside the confines, restrictions, and prejudices that their own corporation imposes on them. They would also have to be effective and forceful enough to enact changes through their corporation to stay in front of the marketplace and to keep the organization growing and healthy. This change in roles and behaviors is huge – but it is not impossible. All that is needed is for the person to have a great understanding of his or her talents, and to take this understanding, and build a strategy around applying these talents to the new role. Without this last step, the chances of success are narrowed considerably.

Taking advantage of your talents

Chapter Six of *Now, Discover Your Strengths* is full of excellent examples of how to take advantage of, and apply, each of the thirty-four talents. Some examples are described below, but refer to the book for a complete description of all the talents.

Achiever: These people are motivated by being busy and by successfully meeting goals. Help them get involved in activities, set measurable goals, and then work toward these goals. Achievers love to work hard, but they are de-motivated if they have to work with slackers. Recognize them for their hard work and achievements, then assign a new task that will keep them extremely busy, and allow them to achieve.

Analytical: These people are very logical; they like to have things explained logically. They like to spend time thinking through issues, and they don't like making snap decisions. They like to have precise data presented to them before a decision is made. They like to look for patterns and trends in data, and accuracy may be more important than schedules.

Belief: Discover their passion and find ways to apply this passion in the work environment. Spend time with these people to ensure they find a way to align personal values to corporate values. Ensure that their values and beliefs are respected.

Command: Put these people in charge when you need results. Involve them in evaluations of processes. Place them in leadership roles, but watch for overbearing leadership, and provide guidance if it occurs. Provide some sensitivity training, so that the leadership style of these people does not appear overbearing or threatening.

Empathy: People with this talent are attuned to the emotions of others. Allow them to evaluate the feelings of personnel within your organization. These people tend to be emotional and need your understanding. Always inquire how they feel about new assignments and new roles. Place them in positions with other optimistic people; putting them together with pessimistic people only depresses them.

Ideation: Give these people roles that take advantage of their creative ideas. Expose them to organizational ideas and present their ideas to the organization. Spend time explaining corporate and technical decisions, showing how and why they make sense.

Intellection: Allow these people time to think. They are energized by thinking and aren't afraid to be challenged in their thinking. These people like to read material, think about it, and discuss their learnings.

Learner: Place these people in fast-changing environments and help them stay current. Allow them to learn new skills and knowledge. Pay for training and track their learning progress. Encourage them to become experts in their fields. Assign mentors to provide technical guidance. Allow them to lead internal focus groups within their areas of expertise.

Maximizer: These people are motivated by making things better, not by fixing things that are broken. Continual problem-solving may be de-motivating. Spend time with them defining their strengths and put them in roles that maximize those strengths. Help them determine career paths that allow them to be top performers and help them advance in their careers.

Relator: Spend time developing trusting, sincere relationships with these people. Don't allow them to change roles frequently, as this often results in lost or broken relationships. If possible, allow these people to build trusting, sincere relationships with the employees you want to retain.

Responsibility: This person will always live up to commitments. They will not let anything get in the way of this. They can be impatient and don't like "slackers" on their team – or others that bring down the quality of the overall product. They are independent self-starters, but they do need to be monitored to ensure their zealousness does not get them into trouble.

I currently have a project manager working for me who has *Achiever* and *Responsibility* talents. We have worked with this individual to define a role that allows him to put these strengths to work and take advantage of these talents every day. He is given projects that are not only technically challenging but commercially challenging as well. This allows him to achieve. He thrives in high-pressure situations, and he always delivers, especially on projects that have penalty clauses for late or poor-quality deliverables. He always completes what is required on time. Periodically, however, he does need to be coached about his people skills. He has walked over people who have stood between him and his ability to meet his defined commitments.

In like fashion, we have also spent some time with another project manager who has Intellection and Analytical talents. This project manager does not want a high-pressure, high-stress environment, although he has worked on projects like this. He prefers a single project with a decent timeline and a well-defined contract. He spends time thinking about the project from all angles including budgets, schedules, resources, scope, contract, and commercial aspects. He is able to handle the situations encountered on the project by running them through different analysis, taking into account all of these aspects. He spends time analyzing these scenarios and picks the best response while balancing the client's expectations, the schedule, and our profitability requirements.

Conclusion

You can see how important it is to understand your own Talent Strength Zone, along with the Talent Strength Zone of your family members, your co-workers, and your company.

When you have developed this understanding, as Buckingham and Clifton state, you can begin to "craft your role to play to your signature talents most of the time." As well, you can help others to do the same. This will truly result in a more productive environment, whether at work or at home.

Summary

1. Talent is a naturally recurring pattern of thought, feeling, or behavior. It is not knowledge or skill.

2. People do not want to pay for average. People only want to pay for above average, so you must build on your strength areas to ensure success.

3. There are thirty-four talent themes in total, but each person has only five primary themes.

4. Primary talents are determined by the age of fifteen. These primary talents cannot be changed.

5. There is no such thing as the perfect talent combination, but there are certain individual talents that are beneficial to certain roles.

6. Dominant talents are important because they represent the areas in which you can achieve the biggest gain with the least pain.

7. The goal of the StrengthsFinder Profile is to identify your dominant talents and inspire you to build in these areas. This is your Talent Strength Zone.

8. Everyone needs to strive to build on their own Talent Strength Zone and to help others identify and work within their Talent Strength Zone.

Application exercise

1. Record your top five talents below as identified by the www.strengthsfinder.com evaluation (or if you are unable to purchase this book, by peer evaluation). This is your Talent Strength Zone.

1	
2	
3	
4	
5	

2. Think about a role that you currently work in.

Write it down. _____

3. How can you be more productive in this role by aligning it around your talents (your Talent Strength Zone)?

4. If you work as part of a team, what are the talents of your team members? Do they know their talents? Are they working in the Talent Strength Zone or do they need to have some guidance to identify their talents and restructure their roles to take advantage of these talents?

Talent self evaluation form

If you cannot purchase *Now, Discover Your Strengths,* have between five and ten close associates, peers, direct reports, and superiors evaluate your talents by selecting what they feel are your top five talents out of the list provided below. In the table below, have them place a star in the empty column next to each of five of your top talents.

Achiever: This talent is illustrated in a quote taken from *The Fred Factor*: "Look to every day as a new day and make each day better than the last. Even on my days off, I have goals, and I feel like I need to get a lot done. If I feel like I wasted the day, I don't sleep quite as well at night."

Activator: Impatient for action – only action leads to performance.

Adaptability: Live for the moment. Able to respond to the demands of the moment and change plans as required.

Analytical: Objective and dispassionate. Theories must be backed with facts.

Arranger: Likes taking complex, multivariable situations, and aligning all the variables until the optimal solution is reached.

Belief: Enduring core values. Typically family-oriented with high ethics. Aaltruistic. Values responsibility.

Command: Likes to take charge of situations. Has no problem in doing so and in letting people know how things really are.

Communication: Energized by public speaking and writing in a way that energizes other people.

Competition: Very aware of the performance of others and must outperform others.

Connectedness: Considerate, caring, and accepting. Bridge builder. Believes that all people are connected.

Context: Looking back to the past to find answers for the present. The past provides knowledge of how things should be handled now.

Deliberative: Careful and cautious. Evaluates risks before acting.

Developer: Sees potential in others and wants to help them develop it.

Discipline: Needs things to be structured and predictable, ordered and planned.

Empathy: Senses the emotions of others. Has the ability to see through the eyes of others.

Fairness: Balance is important. Needs to treat everyone the same way.

Focus: Needs a clear destination. Goal-setting is important.

Futuristic: Is able to perceive or paint the future and loves trying to do this.

Harmony: Helps others find areas for agreement. Is adverse to conflict. Finds common ground between contentious issues.

Ideation: Fascinated with new concepts, with familiar challenges, or with new and disparate phenomena.

Inclusiveness: Needs to include people, not exclude them. Is distressed by seeing people on the outside looking in.

Individualization: Able to observe and identify uniqueness in every individual. Able to identify and pull out strengths in all people.

Input: Inquisitive. A collector.

Intellection: Likes to think. Likes mental activities. Likes to develop ideas or solve problems.

Learner: Loves learning. The process of learning, as opposed to the subject matter, is important.

Maximizer: Taking something strong to something superb, as opposed to moving from substandard to above average. Excellence is the measure.

Positivity: Generous with praise and quick to smile. Lighthearted optimist.

Relator: Is pulled toward familiar people. Is not necessarily shy in front of strangers but gets a great deal of pleasure from close friends.

Responsibility: Takes ownership for anything that is committed to. Follows through to completion.

Restorative: Loves to solve problems. Enjoys analyzing symptoms and finding a solution.

Self-assurance: Self-confidence. Has faith in own strengths and in own judgment.

Significance: Needs to be recognized for accomplishments. Wants to push others to achievement and recognition.

Strategic: Able to navigate though obstacles and to chart the best route between two points.

Woo (Winning Others Over): Enjoys the challenge of meeting new people and getting them to like you.

Skills and Knowledge

· 6 ·

A skill is designed to make the secrets of the best easily transferable. If you learn a skill, it will help you get a little better, but it will not cover for a lack of talent.

**- Now, Discover Your Strengths *by*
Marcus Buckingham and Donald Clifton**

Successfully intelligent people figure out their strengths and their weaknesses, and then find ways to capitalize on their strengths...and to correct for or remedy their weaknesses.

- Successful Intelligence by Robert J. Sternberg

As we learned in the last chapter on talents, *skills* are the steps of an activity and *knowledge* is facts and lessons learned. What we want to ensure is that we use our knowledge of our values, personality, and talent Strength Zones to maximize our effectiveness. One way to do this is to ensure that we develop knowledge and skills within our Overall Strength Zone. This will help to ensure that we are not learning skills or knowledge that we cannot apply in the most effective method possible.

Skills

Literally thousands of skills are required to complete the activities required of us today. Zig Ziglar stated in one of his CD-based seminars that there are more than fifty thousand registered occupations in the United States. Each one of these fifty thousand occupations comes with its own set of skills.

On Lilongwe, we had many different types of skill sets, ranging from project management to cost control to technical programming to document writing to cabinet design to cabinet fabrication. Each of these skill sets is a combination of many skills, some of which are in areas of specialization. For example, a small subset of a project manager's skills could be depicted as follows:

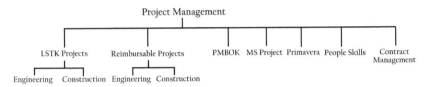

Likewise, a small subset of a control system programmer's various skill sets could be depicted as follows:

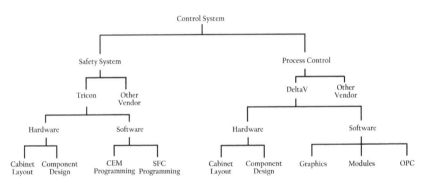

In each of these examples, potentially hundreds of skills are not shown. Each person may not have all of these skills, and one person may possess more skills in a particular area than in another area. For example, a safety system programmer may possess more skills in the area of Cause and Effect Matrix (CEM) programming than in Sequential Function Chart (SFC) programming and may therefore gravitate to this role on projects.

How do you determine what you are skilled at? How can you quantify this?

Printed with permission

HARVARD BUSINESS REVIEW, NOV. 2005

"ACTUALLY HE HAS NO JOB SKILLS, BUT WE KEEP HIM ON BOARD TO FEED OFF HIS UNCANNY LUCK."

Many tools and methods exist for measuring your skills. Skill-based tests are the most common. Some corporations make a profit by providing assessments for the business world and for the academic world. These tests range from in-person spoken tests, to written tests, to online Internet-based tests. At least one website is dedicated to online quizzes (www.quizbox.com), although many of the tests have no scientific basis.

From kindergarten to grade twelve, a student's skill level is assessed against a national, provincial or state standard. This assessment is completed using assignments and tests. As the students move from grade twelve to college or university, the testing becomes more serious. In Canada, students are assessed using grade twelve departmental exams. In the United States, students are assessed with SAT tests (Scholastic Aptitude Tests). Their skills in each of the core subjects are measured by these tests, and their academic future depends on how well they perform. Unfortunately, according to Robert J. Sternberg in *Successful*

Intelligence, many of these tests are flawed. What is really being measured, says Sternberg, is the student's ability in test-taking.

Assessment by testing continues as students progress through college or university. In fact, this method of measuring specific academic skill sets is the backbone of any technical program. The perception in academia is that someone who scores well on tests will be successful in future endeavors; and someone who scores poorly will struggle. Sternberg, however, says this is not true. "Successfully intelligent people defy negative expectations, even when these expectations arise from low scores on IQ (Intelligence Quotient) or similar tests. They do not let other people's assessments stop them from achieving their goals. They find their path and then pursue it, realizing that there will be obstacles along the way and that surmounting these obstacles is part of their challenge."

Sternberg goes on to say that successfully intelligent people capitalize on their intellectual strengths and compensate for and correct their weaknesses. Parents, schools, and the workplace need to support the development of successful intelligence in whatever ways they can and to view intellectual abilities as dynamic and flexible rather than as static and fixed.

According to Sternberg, "**Successfully intelligent people figure out their strengths and their weaknesses, and then find ways to capitalize on their strengths...and to correct for or remedy their weaknesses...**" (Emphasis added.)

To achieve success, then, you first need to understand your strengths and weaknesses. This understanding will probably not come from skills tests.

Assessment in sports is somewhat easier than in academics. Athletes are assessed by how fast they can skate, how fast they can run forty yards, how many goals they can score, how many hits they make, how many tackles they complete, how many assists they earn, and on and on. People make a good living recording these statistics on each player in every sport. The statistics for each player are compared against the performances of past and current players, and each player is rated based on these statistics. Teams line up to draft or sign the best players. In some sports, this process starts with players as young as fourteen years old.

In the business world, the methods of evaluating your skill sets are somewhat limited. This is primarily due to the fact that many of the activities completed by business people involve personal time management and soft skills (people skills). Measuring these skills is somewhat subjective, not an exact science. However, most skill assessments in the business world are still valuable, regardless of how difficult it can be to get highly accurate results. They do indicate strengths and weaknesses. The most popular tests for measuring an executive's skills are 360º evaluations.

360º evaluations

When performed correctly, the 360º evaluation involves people from all areas of your professional life: bosses, peers, and those for whom you are responsible. Each person within these groups sees you performing a different role and may judge your performance differently. To get a well-rounded assessment, participants in each category are asked to assess your skill level in predetermined categories. The skill categories differ between assessment companies, but the end goal is still the same – to assess the executive's skill level and to define patterns of strength and weakness.

Many of the originators of these tests believe that you must be strong in all skill sets. Where weaknesses are identified, you must work hard to improve. But this is where I disagree with the testers. Although I agree that weaknesses must be compensated so that they don't become liabilities, I do not believe that people should waste time trying to improve areas of weakness unless that weakness is an issue of attitude, relationships, or discipline. If you have an identified area of weakness, I suggest that you hire someone who has a dominant strength in this area and allow that person to handle this work.

My approach to the 360º evaluations is to compare them to your Strength Zone. In what skills do you have the highest scores? Do these skills match your Strength Zone? How can you develop your skills to build on your Strength Zone? How can you use your Strength Zone to develop skills?

What you may find is that your highest scores on skills correlates with the skills that fall into your Strength Zone (as defined by your values, personality, and talents). However, don't feel bad if you don't score as high as you expected in an area. Many people have not developed their Strength Zone because they had not defined their zones. Also, as much as science is used to build these 360º evaluations, they can still be subjective and subject to error.

A good example of this is the score I received recently in "Strategic Skills" on a Lominger Leadership Architect© 360º evaluation. This skill set scored dead last out of all skill sets due to low scores on two specific skill categories:

- Cluster B: Making Complex Decisions
- Cluster C: Creating the New and Different

These are two sets of skills that I should be good at when my values, personality, and talents are considered (my personality profile combination is *Creative* and my identified talents include *Maximizer, Ideation, Learner,* and *Achiever*). However, my 360º evaluation facilitator pointed out that most of the people who scored me low in these areas were not aware of what I was doing on a management level. They were used to my work at the detailed programming level, work that I had to leave behind when I moved into a project manager role.

After moving into the project manager position, I began facing decisions that were just as complex as at the programming level. I had to balance project and corporate finance with project scope and schedule, and balance this with client satisfaction. Add to this mix personnel issues, passport and visa issues, language barriers and culture issues. At the same time, I was creating project management tools that did not exist, personnel policies that were required for overseas work, project standards, and so on. All of these decisions and processes were complex, requiring a lot of creativity. However, most of this work was not visible to the people who provided the lower scores. They only saw my lack of involvement at the programming level. This is also a good example of why these 360º evaluations should always be administered by a qualified facilitator.

Many of these evaluations are available. The two that I am familiar with are the Lominger Leadership Architect© and an assessment package from the Center for Creative Leadership called SkillScope©. Skill sets from the Lominger Leadership Architect© package are outlined below.

Lominger ©

The Lominger© model developed by Michael M. Lombardo and Robert W. Eichinger defines the areas of skills that one can be proficient in as the following:

<u>**Strategic skills**</u>

Cluster A: Understanding the Business
- Business Acumen
- Functional/Technical Skills
- Technical Learning

Cluster B: Making Complex Decisions
- Decision Quality
- Intellectual Horsepower
- Learning on the Fly
- Problem Solving

Cluster C: Creating the New and the Different
- Dealing with Ambiguity
- Creativity
- Innovation Management
- Perspective
- Strategic Agility

<u>**Operating skills**</u>

Cluster D: Keeping on Point
- Timely Decision Making
- Priority Setting

Cluster E: Getting Organized
- Organizing
- Planning
- Time Management

Cluster F: Getting Work Done Through Others
- Delegation
- Developing Direct Reports and Others
- Directing Others
- Informing
- Managing Work and Measuring Work

Cluster G: Managing Work Processes
- Process Management
- Managing Through Systems
- Total Work Systems

Courage

Cluster H: Dealing With Trouble
- Command Skills
- Conflict Management
- Confronting Direct Reports
- Managerial Courage
- Standing Alone

Cluster I: Making Tough People Calls
- Hiring and Staffing
- Sizing Up People

Energy and drive

Cluster J: Focusing on the Bottom Line
- Action Oriented
- Perseverance
- Drive For Results

Organizational positioning

Cluster K: Being Organizationally Savvy
- Organizational Agility
- Political Savvy

Cluster L: Communicating Effectively
- Presentation Skills
- Written Communications

Cluster M: Managing Up
- Career Ambition
- Comfort Around Higher Management

Personal and interpersonal

Cluster N: Relating Skills
- Approachability
- Interpersonal Savvy

Cluster O: Caring About Others
- Caring About Direct Reports
- Compassion

Cluster P: Managing Diverse Relationships
- Boss Relationships
- Customer Focus
- Managing Diversity
- Fairness to Direct Reports
- Peer Relationships
- Understanding Others

Cluster Q: Inspiring Others
- Motivating Others
- Negotiating
- Building Effective Teams
- Managing Vision and Purpose

Cluster R: Acting With Honor and Character
- Ethics and Values
- Integrity and Trust

Cluster S: Being Open and Receptive
- Composure
- Humor
- Listening
- Patience
- Personal Disclosure

Cluster T: Demonstrating Personal Flexibility
- Dealing With Paradox

- Personal Learning
- Self Development
- Self Knowledge

Cluster U: Balancing Work/Life
- Work/Life Balance

My employer adopted the Lominger system so I was able to go through the 360º evaluation process. My scores out of five were as follows:

Skill	Score
Strategic skills	**3.67**
Cluster A: Understanding the Business	3.67
Cluster B: Making Complex Decisions	3.78
Cluster C: Creating the New and the Different	3.56
Operating skills	**4.22**
Cluster D: Keeping on Point	4.22
Cluster E: Getting Organized	4.22
Cluster F: Getting Work Done Through Others	4.22
Cluster G: Managing Work Processes	4.22
Courage	**4.17**
Cluster H: Dealing with Trouble	4.22
Cluster I: Making Tough People Calls	4.11
Energy and drive	**4.00**
Cluster J: Focusing on the Bottom Line	4.00
Organizational positioning	**3.96**
Cluster K: Being Organizationally Savvy	3.89
Cluster L: Communicating Effectively	4.11
Cluster M: Managing Up	3.89
Personal and interpersonal	**3.89**
Cluster N: Relating Skills	3.67
Cluster O: Caring About Others	3.67
Cluster P: Managing Diverse Relationships	3.89
Cluster Q: Inspiring Others	4.11
Cluster R: Acting With Honor and Character	4.33
Cluster S: Being Open and Receptive	3.89
Cluster T: Demonstrating Personal Flexibility	3.78
Cluster U: Balancing Work/Life	3.78

How does this relate to my Strength Zone?

How does this match my values, personality, and talents Strength Zones? If you recall from the previous chapters, one of my talents is *Achiever*, one of my values is *Courage*, and one of my personality traits is *Challenger*.

Look at these three elements: *Achiever, Courage* and *Challenger*. These seem to fit with Cluster H: Dealing with Trouble, and with Cluster I: Making Tough People Calls.

I value achievement.

Achievement is part of my personality trait, and it is one of my talents. This probably explains why I scored high on the energy and drive section of the Lominger test. I love a challenge and value courage, so I am able to handle tough people calls and dealing with trouble efficiently.

My highest skill score on the Lominger test was in operating skills. This includes keeping on point, getting organized, getting work done through others, and managing work processes. At first glance, this does not necessarily fit with my values, personality, or talents, but take a closer look. I can use my knowledge of my *Achiever* strength to restructure my role to achieve a high score in keeping on point and getting organized. If I don't ensure that I am on point and organized, how can I achieve? I am extremely motivated to be focused and organized because if I am not, I will not be able to reach and exceed my goals.

One of my talents is *Maximizer*. For me to work smoothly and efficiently, I need to build on existing work. I don't like to start from scratch. I am motivated to manage work processes that already are in place, as I like to work with and build from an existing base. This also fits in with my *Achiever* traits. I cannot achieve everything that is possible unless I can work efficiently with established work processes, maybe even improving them where possible.

Someone who scores high in these same skills may not have the same Strength Zone. Most won't. The trick is to understand your Strength Zone and to determine how to restructure your role or approach in order to improve the needed skill. For example, a person with a Talent

Strength Zone of *Commander* might be more likely to have a higher skills score in Dealing with Trouble than someone with a Talent Strength Zone of *Competition*. However, the individual with the *Competition* talent could determine how to improve in Dealing with Trouble by taking advantage of his or her Strength Zone. The person might, for example, build a system to improve and measure employee satisfaction in the trouble areas and self-compete to constantly improve or maintain these scores.

What did I do about the low skill scores?

What about my lowest scores? How can I leverage my values, personality, and talents Strength Zones to improve in these areas? This is assuming, of course, that improvement is required. In some cases, I can hire someone who is excellent in my areas of weakness. That will allow me to continue building on my strength areas, knowing that my areas of weakness are covered by someone I trust. However, let's assume that I don't have this luxury and that I need to improve my skill in Creating New and Different, which happens to be my lowest score. What can I do?

This is what I did. In looking again at my personality assessment, I saw that one of my profile traits is *Creative*. I also looked again at my talents. One of my top five is *Ideation*, which means I have a fascination with new concepts and the application of these concepts to different situations. How, I wondered, can I use these Strength Zones to improve my Creating New and Different skill?

I began to spend time on Friday afternoons reviewing my week. I looked more closely at the various situations I had encountered during the week, evaluating these situations – and my response – to see where I could have improved my performance.

I reviewed the concepts taught in the book *The Five Faces of Genius* by Annett Moser-Wellman, and I used these concepts to re-evaluate my activities over the week. *The Five Faces of Genius* explains creativity and how people approach problems. It provides a process for individuals to classify themselves into one of five creative types:

- **Seer**: the ability to visualize a solution

- **Observer**: the ability to notice extreme detail around you and to use this to define a solution

- **Alchemist**: the ability to connect diverse domains into a solution

- **Fool**: the ability to consider the seemingly absurd to define a solution

- **Sage**: the ability to simplify a complicated situation and provide a solution

The book defines each of these creativity types in detail and explains how anyone can begin to use all five of the creativity types to become even more creative. Answering the questions in the brief profile provided in the book, I discovered I was a *Seer* and an *Observer*. I spent time reviewing the benefits of these two creative profiles, and then I spent more time understanding the *Alchemist*, *Fool*, and *Sage* profiles and how they work. I now consciously apply some of the techniques from all of these creative types to many of the problems that I have to solve on a day-to-day basis. I also bring other people in to help me solve some of these problems if they have creative strengths in areas of my creative weaknesses.

It is extremely important to note that the 360° evaluations must be administered by a properly trained and qualified individual. Failure to do this (if you try to build your own evaluation and select people to provide feedback, for example) can, and will, result in a multitude of problems ranging from inaccuracy because those you selected are worried about repercussions to human resource issues because of repercussions. A properly trained facilitator will keep test inputs or sources anonymous and will provide the results in a properly formatted report, complete with statistical analysis showing the assessee's skill strengths and weaknesses, along with required areas for improvement.

Other skill-based tests

Many other skill-based tests are available to help users define their strengths and weaknesses in many specialized areas. Some of these tests are quite formalized, and others are quite informal. I have provided one informal example below of a leadership skill assessment that I found valuable.

Bill Hybels

In his book *Courageous Leadership*, author Bill Hybels provides a definition of required leadership skills. If you are in a position of leadership, it is well worth your time to evaluate yourself from top strength to bottom strength. It is also worth the time to have someone who works closely with you provide an assessment of your leadership capabilities and to discuss any differences of opinion. As mentioned earlier, most people assume a leadership role in some area of their lives. It could be as a parent, Sunday school teacher, charity organizer, or community sports coach. The set of skills listed below could also be beneficial to you.

1. **Visionary leadership**: These leaders have a crystal-clear picture in mind of what the future holds.

2. **Directional leadership**: These leaders have the ability to chart the course. They can choose the correct path for the organization as it approaches a critical intersection.

3. **Strategic leadership**: These leaders have the ability to take an exciting vision and break it into a series of sequential and achievable steps. They can form a game plan that everyone can relate to and buy into. They can align all subgroups of an organization.

4. **Managing leadership**: These leaders have the ability to organize people, processes and resources to achieve a mission. They can bring order out of chaos.

5. **Motivational leadership**: These leaders have the ability to keep the team fired up. They provide the right kind of inspiration to each person.

6. **Shepherding leadership**: These leaders have the ability to build a team slowly, love them deeply, nurture them, support them, and listen to them patiently.

7. **Team-building leadership**: These leaders understand vision and how to achieve it. They have insight into people and can

successfully select and develop the right people with the right attitudes and chemistry, and place these people together in the correct positions on the correct teams.

8. **Entrepreneurial leadership**: These leaders possess some or all of the other styles but are most successful in startup mode. They need to create and develop something new all of the time. Once it is up and running, they will move on to start something else.

9. **Re-engineering leadership**: These leaders are at their best when placed in turnaround situations. They thrive on fixing troubled situations.

10. **Bridge-building leadership**: These leaders have the ability to bring together many different interest groups. They are diplomats, skilled at negotiation and compromise.

I had a number of people evaluate me against Bill Hybels' leadership skills. I discovered that my top five leadership strengths are as follows:

1) Strategic leadership
2) Managing leadership
3) Directional leadership
4) Entrepreneurial leadership
5) Visionary and team-building (tied for fifth place)

How does this relate to my Strength Zone?

How does this relate to my values, personality, and talent Strength Zones? Because one of my Strength Zones is *Achiever*, I need to be able to understand exactly where my business is and to set specific goals for the future. I base these goals on many factors, both known and predicted. I then set strategies in place that allow me and my team members to frequently measure progress against these goals and to adjust our strategies as required.

This does not mean that only someone with an Achiever Strength Zone will be strong in strategic leadership. It does mean that you have to understand your Strength Zone and work on redefining your roles around your Strength Zone to make yourself as effective as possible.

What it also means is that you need to work with the people around you to take advantage of their Strength Zone. For example, what if you had a role that required strategic leadership, but you could not figure out how to use your Strength Zone in this role? One solution would be to put someone on your team who does have a Strategic Leadership Strength Zone into that role.

What did I do about the low skill scores?

I wasn't worried about the low skill scores on this test. If I'm no good at something like Bridge-Building Leadership I will avoid doing this myself. If I get into a situation where this is required, I will look for someone I know and trust who is competent in Bridge-Building Leadership. It is not always necessary to improve in low skill areas, or in areas of weakness unless, as mentioned earlier, these areas of weakness are in attitude, relationships, or discipline.

Goal of the skill assessment

As we have seen, many skills tests are available. Any skills assessment tool will help you evaluate your skills. Use these tools to identify where you can build skills that correlate with your Strength Zone or where you can use your Strength Zone to build your skills. For businesspeople, the most effective of these tests is a properly administered 360° evaluation.

In progressing through the skills-based assessments, it is important to realize that most are not value-based, personality-based, or talent-based. These are skills. Skills are activities defined by steps. Skills can be learned. In fact, skills *must* be learned as you attempt to build your Strength Zone.

Take a skills test

Go to the Lominger website and get set up for a 360° evaluation. Refer to www.StrengthZone.ca for website links. When you receive the results, analyze them according to your Strength Zone.

Do you have high scores in skills related to your Strength Zone according to your values, personality, and talents? If you do not, you need to begin building these skills into strengths. This is done by:

- Taking courses
- Reading books
- Finding a mentor
- Hiring an executive coach
- Books on CD
- Seminars in person
- Seminars on CD

I set development goals for myself each year. For example:

- I read, as a minimum, one book a month
- I listen to John C. Maxwell's MIC CD training each month
- I listen to one book on CD each month
- I attend a minimum of two training seminars each year
- I host a minimum of six training seminars each year on topics I've learned about at seminars or through my own study
- I try to arrange for lunch once a month with someone who is successful in his or her industry. I ask questions and try to learn as much as possible

For those of you that are skeptical on the value of training and skills building, a recent study completed by Robert Zernsky and Susan Shaman of the University of Pennsylvania showed the following:

- A ten percent increase in corporate spending for training led to an 8.5 percent increase in corporate productivity

- A ten percent increase in corporate spending on capital expenditures led to a 3.8 percent increase in corporate productivity

Although this study was done at the corporate level and shows how training employees results in a higher gain in productivity than does capital expenditure, you can easily leverage this insight in your personal training. A small increase in the personal time you spend in training will greatly increase your productivity, both on and off the job.

Knowledge

Knowledge consists of two components:

- **Factual knowledge** – gained by formal training; typically consists of traditional classroom learning environments, reading, seminars, and on-the-job training

- **Experiential knowledge** – gained through real-life experiences, as well as by learning from the experiences of other people

Factual knowledge is typically associated with particular degrees or training programs. Academic qualifications such as a B.Sc., M.B.A., or Ph.D. are typically associated with bodies of knowledge. These can be further broken down into disciplines, such as electrical engineering, medicine, law, and so on. When you have earned such a designation, there is a certain expectation that you are in possession of a common body of knowledge.

Experiential knowledge can be illustrated by thinking of someone living in a tropical climate who has never seen snow. If this person reads about the life of someone living in a cold northern climate, the reader may have gained factual knowledge about temperature scales, wind chill, and snowstorms, but this person has no experiential knowledge – unless, of course, he or she takes a trip to Prudhoe Bay, Alaska in January!

As mentioned at the beginning of this chapter, knowledge can be defined as "facts and lessons learned" and skills can be defined as "steps of an activity." Skills are established by the application of acquired knowledge. One must build up knowledge in an area before skills in this area can be acquired. However, just because one has knowledge in an area does not mean that he or she is skilled in that area. For example, an engineer who graduates from university with a B.Sc. has a certain body of knowledge, but a limited skill set. This engineer's skills become developed after entering the workforce and being guided by a mentor through real-life applications of knowledge. This engineer can also begin to experience what was studied in school, and thus start to acquire experiential knowledge.

Conclusion

The areas in which you can build your knowledge are probably infinite. However, to maximize your effectiveness, you need to concentrate on building your knowledge in your areas of defined strength. This knowledge must then be used to establish or enhance the required skills. First you need to define your Strength Zone, then you need to determine how you can build on this Strength Zone by increasing your knowledge and skills.

Summary

1. Knowledge is facts and lessons learned.

2. Skills are the steps of an activity or the application of acquired knowledge.

3. Take a skills test using a properly administered 360° evaluation.

4. Consider your Strength Zone and determine how to increase your skill competencies and how to learn new skills within your Strength Zone. Decide which skills are outside your strength areas, and develop a plan to deal with these (remove yourself from this area or hire someone to assist).

5. Build knowledge in the areas of your strengths.

6. Apply this acquired knowledge to build skills in identified skill areas.

Application exercise

1. Assess your skills as a leader using Bill Hybels' model. In the chart below, rate each skill from one to ten (with one being the highest).

Leadership Skill	Your Rating	Associate Rating
Visionary		
Directional		
Strategic		
Managing		
Motivational		
Shepherding		
Team-building		
Entrepreneurial		
Re-engineering		
Bridge-building		

2. Have someone else assess your skills as a leader using Bill Hybels' model.

3. Is there a correlation between these two assessments?

4. How can you use your knowledge of your Strength Zone to enhance these skills?

5. How can you use these skills to enhance your Strength Zone?

6. Arrange to have a properly administered 360° evaluation.

7. How can you use your knowledge of your Strength Zone to enhance these identified skills?

8. How can you use these skills to enhance your Strength Zone?

The Intersection

· 7 ·

God is weaving a glorious tapestry from our lives. Sometimes we see only the frayed threads underneath. We need to look from heaven and see the beauty of what the Lord is fashioning from all the loose ends.

- Kathy Self

Having conceived of his purpose, a person should mentally mark out a straight pathway to its achievement, looking neither to the right nor left.

- As a Man Thinketh by James Allen

"Look straight ahead, and fix your eyes on what lies before you. Mark out a straight path for your feet; then stick to the path and stay safe."

- Proverbs 4:25, 26 by Solomon

Values, personality, and talents – these are important components of who we are. They must be identified before we can begin the process of finding our Overall Strength Zone. When they are first identified, they appear as fragments of a puzzle or as the frayed threads of a tapestry. These frayed threads – our values, personality, and talents – are woven together to form the unique and beautify tapestry that defines each of us. Identifying this tapestry and understanding its intricacies allows us to reassess all areas of our lives and to realign these areas in a manner that better fits us. It allows us to live up to our ultimate potential.

By now, you should have completed the values assessment, DISC evaluation, and StrengthsFinder profile. From these activities, you should have a good idea of your Values Strength Zone, Personality Strength Zone, and Talents Strength Zone. By themselves, each of these evaluation techniques offers valuable insights into how you operate and where your strengths lie. You should have learned a great deal about yourself and your strengths just from reading these chapters and doing these exercises.

Examples of how to apply your values, personality, and talents have been provided so that you can begin to make changes in your life, to become more efficient and more productive. Emphasis was also placed on helping others through this same process.

We have talked about skills and knowledge – how they are measured and how we should strive to build our knowledge and skills in our Strength Zone. Conversely, we have discussed using our Strength Zone to build our skills and knowledge.

However, we have not yet talked about bringing all of the pieces of information together and forming one view of our Strength Zone. I believe that when we combine these three sets of data into one picture, it becomes a powerful illustration of where our Overall Strength Zone lies. We can take this information and begin to build on our Strength Zone. We can begin to adjust our role at work, taking advantage of our Strength Zone, and starting to work at becoming more effective and efficient.

This will allow you, as John Eldredge says, to discover your heart's desire and the purpose to your life. It will help lead you to that place where you can truly say, "This is what I was made for!"

Union of sets

The following diagram shows a simple mathematical concept called the union of sets. It indicates the overlapping area, or common area, between three otherwise independent circles.

If we name each of the circles after one of the areas we have been studying – values, personality, and talents – we see that the three areas in the center of the diagram overlap each other. This is the area of concentrated strength. It is the area where you will be the strongest.

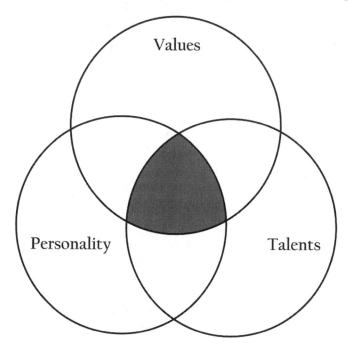

This is a key concept in the process of defining your Overall Strength Zone and maximizing your strengths. Many people struggle all their lives to maximize their effectiveness by concentrating on only one of the circles – talents, for example. They understand that they have talents in certain areas, and they forget about what they value and how their personality adds to, or subtracts from, their effectiveness.

Take the example of Mickey Mantle given earlier in this book. Mantle relied on his physical talents. He never took into account his personality or his values or how they combined to form his Overall Strength Zone. This ultimately resulted in Mantle never reaching his full potential. Similarly, our dedicated C-type (DISC profile) engineers relied on their technical talent and ignored their personality and values. They became great technical resources but limited their usefulness, as they were unable to get along properly with others.

Some people understand that their talents must be maximized in conjunction with their personality (union of two circles), but they forget about their values. My point is this: you cannot become the best you can be without focusing on the intersection of the three key areas. This intersection is your Overall Strength Zone.

Unlike mathematics and the union of sets, what we are doing here is not an exact science with empirical formulas. This process can be subjective – some interpretation and refining may be required as you define your strength areas. For example, the words that you use to describe your personality are not necessarily definite in the same way that a number is defined. Creativity, for example, can be described by other words such as ingenuity, originality, imagination, and inspiration. As such, creativity is comprised of many different facets.

What follows is an example of my own profile and how I was able to use the union of sets method to identify my Overall Strength Zone.

My Profile

The following example uses my values, personality profile, and talents to arrive at the completed union of sets.

My six most important values (Values Strength Zone): *Faith/Religion, Family, Integrity, Wisdom, Achievement*, and *Courage*.

My DISC profile has classified me as a high D and my secondary as a C (classic profile of an engineer!). My DISC combination profile is *Challenger*. My Personality Strength Zone can be summarized by the following words. These words were taken from the written description of my profile type that was provided by PeopleKeys: *Creative, Dominant, Loves Challenge, Competitive, Solves Problems, Impatient to Start, Planning Ability, Achievement*, and *Change Oriented*.

According to the StrengthFinders test, my Talent Strength Zone is *Maximizer, Ideation, Learner, Achiever*, and *Belief*.

All of this information can be summarized in the following chart.

Values	DISC	Talents
Faith/religion	Creative	Maximizer
Family	Competitive	Ideation
Integrity	Impatient to start	Learner
Wisdom	Planning ability	Achiever
Achievement	Achievement	Belief
Courage	Change oriented	
	Dominant	
	Challenge	
	Solve problems	

Transfer this data from the chart to the "union of sets" and we have the following diagram.

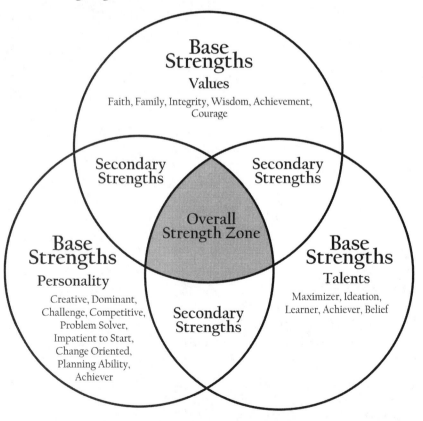

The next diagram indicates the union of all three sets.

According to this model, my Overall Strength Zone – the common areas between my values, personality, and talents are:

1. Achiever

2. Creative, Problem Solving, Learner, Ideation

Note that I have combined *Creative*, *Problem Solving*, *Learner*, and *Ideation* as one primary strength. This is because they all seem to define or point at the same basic strength. This is an illustration of what we talked about in the previous section, where I said this process can be somewhat subjective. Some interpretation is required.

My secondary strengths, comprised of the remaining overlapping strengths between two circles, can be defined as follows:

1. Wisdom
2. Problem solving
3. Dominant
4. Courage
5. Faith
6. Planning ability
7. Change oriented

My remaining base strengths can be defined as follows:

1. Integrity
2. Maximizer
3. Impatient to start
4. Competitive

What can we do with this information?

The intent of this exercise is to help you identify your Overall Strength Zone. After you have defined your Overall Strength Zone, you can spend time developing further in this area by building your knowledge and skills. You must also look at redefining your role(s) to take advantage of your Overall Strength Zone. This process will allow you to become more efficient and effective in your life and in your career. It will provide much more satisfaction as you move toward that point in your life where you can say, "This is what I was made for!"

This process will also help you identify areas that are not strength areas for you. Once you have identified these areas, at work or at home, you may want to rethink your role or position. The goal is to place yourself in your Strength Zone.

The process also defines some weaknesses that you may have. To remove yourself from these areas of weakness, you will have to rethink your role or position. After you begin to help others through this process, you may be able to recruit people who have strengths that supplement your weaknesses.

This whole process can be boiled down to three stages, as shown in the diagram below:

Stage One determines what your greatest potential strength areas are (your Strength Zone).

Stage Two consists of building your knowledge and skills in the areas of your strengths, thus making them stronger.

Stage Three takes a detailed look at all of your roles to determine how you can best take advantage of your Strength Zone and maximize your effectiveness in your roles.

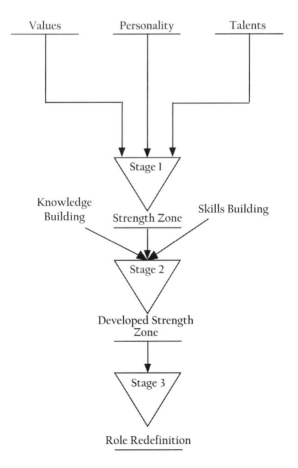

For example, my Overall Strength Zone includes *Achiever*, *Creative*, and *Learner*. This is the output from Stage One in the diagram above. In Stage Two, knowledge and skills building, I could:

1. Take time management or task management courses so I can get more out of the day than the day gets out of me. This would build on my Achiever Strength Zone.

2. Take speed-reading courses to learn how to read and digest material faster. This would build on my Learner Strength Zone.

3. Subscribe to an executive book club that summarizes the most popular business books each month. This would let me review more material in a shorter period of time, building on my Learner, Achiever, and Creative Strength Zones.

4. Take a course or read a book on how to think more creatively (such as *The Five Faces of Genius* by Annette Moser-Wellman). This would build on my Creative Strength Zone.

In Stage Three of the process, I would take each of my roles and adapt them to take advantage of my Strength Zone.

For example, one of my roles was to recruit new employees and to properly resource existing employees into the appropriate positions. If I were to look at my Achiever Strength Zone for this exercise, I could do the following:

i. Hiring of resources: *Establish a success ratio in hiring successful candidates versus those unsuccessful. My goal was to hire the proper person for the proper job with as low a turnover as possible.*

ii. Placement of internal resources into an appropriate position on a project: *Establish an employee utilization rate that measured the number of productive hours that could be charged to a client versus the number of hour that were charged to overhead because people were not being productive in their assigned position.*

Living and working in your Strength Zone

Living and working in your Strength Zone can be compared to using a set of camera lenses. These Strength Zone lenses are composed of a values lens, a personality lens, and a talents lens, although not necessarily in that order.

The user of a camera is able to use different lenses to focus properly in different situations and environments. As the situation changes, the photographer simply adjusts the camera's lenses and refocuses to take an optimum photograph. The camera interprets everything through its lenses. If the lens only allows photos to be taken in one situation, such as the lenses of many cheap, disposable cameras, the photographer is extremely limited (although even this camera can be useful within its limited environment).

Similarly, each person is like a camera. The "person-camera" sees everything and interprets everything it encounters through its unique lens system. These values, talents, and personality lenses can be adjusted and focused in response to local conditions, or they can be set to operate in only one state. Like a photographer adjusting the lens to get an optimum photograph in each unique situation, a person-camera is able to adjust the values, personality, and talents lenses to fit the current situation and environment.

This does not mean that you sell out your values to fit the situation. We discussed this back in Chapter Two. Selling out – violating your values to fit the current situation – is absolutely wrong. You should never do this. However, we did talk about being able to align (or share) your values with the values of a corporation, or a project, or, in this case, the situation or the environment. This has to be done so that your basic values are not being violated, while at the same time, you are in alignment with the values required by the situation.

For example, refer back to the values of the Disney Corporation: *safety, courtesy, show,* and *efficiency.* Most family-oriented people would not choose *efficiency* over spending time with family. However, working at Disney does not force a family-oriented person to violate the value of *family.* It simply means that the person's values must be aligned with Disney's values while at work. They are sharing values.

Disney understands that an employee may have to leave work should a family member become injured or sick. The company would never force that employee to remain working so it could operate a show more efficiently. Disney understands that that would violate all its values (*safety, courtesy, show,* and *efficiency* would all be negatively affected due to the employee's concern about the family member). This is what shared values are all about.

Do you see what is happening here? The person working at Disney is adjusting the focal point of his or her values lens to align with Disney's values. Instead of violating his or her values, the person is sharing Disney's values. The person still has the option of adjusting the values lens back to the *family* focal point should there be a need.

If you decide not to adjust your values focal point as appropriate, you will be more prone to interpersonal values-based conflicts and personal-versus-corporate values conflicts, severely limiting your overall effectiveness.

Similarly, you have the ability to adjust your personality lens based on the situation or on the environment. You can make a decision based on your knowledge of the situation and adjust your personality lens needs to meet the needs of a D type of interaction, or an I, S, or C type of interaction. Changing your own personality lens to match another person's personality type helps you to understand the situation and environment much more efficiently and accurately. Failure to adjust your own personality focal point will result in more interpersonal conflict and severely limit your overall effectiveness.

As for the talent lens, the goal is to tune it to its optimum setting by discovering your talents and working to develop them as near to perfection as you can. You will then be able to use your talents to properly focus and interpret the outside world. You will be using each of your talents as the situation and environment dictates.

Unlike a camera, however, people are able to respond to the outside world when prompted or required. This response is governed by the same set of lenses used to interpret inputs from the outside world. Again, the exact order of the lenses is not important. What is important is that each person's response is run through the values, personality, and talents lenses. People take input from the outside world, focus this input through their values, personality, and talents lenses using their knowledge of the situation, then process these inputs and respond to the outside world. In doing so, they again adjust their values, personality, and talents lenses to match the environment in which they are communicating.

This process is illustrated by the diagram below.

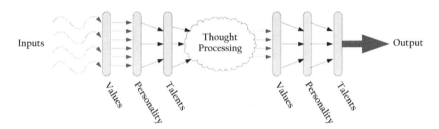

Being a process control engineer for so many years, I just have to show the following diagram illustrating the closed-loop control process I have just described.

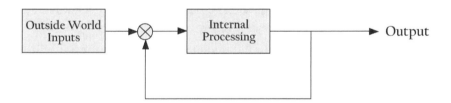

Although the human mind is so much more complicated than this and able to process so many inputs and outputs at the same time, the process of receiving an input from the outside world, processing that input, producing an output, and then continually adjusting the output based on the changing situation can be shown in the simple diagram below.

Note that the "Internal Processing" box contains the set of lenses described above.

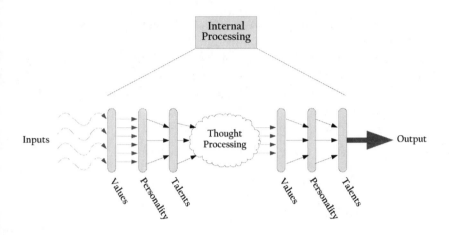

These changing situations include different roles that you may have. A role can be as simple as a position assigned to you within an organization or as complex as working within a position on a particular day in a particular meeting with a particular client negotiating for a particular contract. You need to be aware of your own values, your corporate values, your client's values, and the personalities and talents of all the people involved, both in the meeting and available to you within your organization. All this data can be used to continually adjust the focal points of your lenses as you attempt to be as effective and efficient as possible in your changing roles.

So how does this relate to your Strength Zone? Every person has a particular focal point for each of their lenses. This focal point allows them to work in absolute excellence. Finding these focal settings and the resulting state of excellence is usually called "being in the zone." I call it your Strength Zone. It is comprised of your values, personality, and talents Strength Zones. When you are working in this zone, you can experience a state close to euphoria, with everything seeming to come together perfectly. Just working or being in this state can be energizing, increasing your effectiveness and efficiency.

This can be compared to a great day at the golf course (I haven't had one yet, but I'm told they exist). Have you ever experienced a day where you can't hit a bad shot even if you try? Even when you shank a shot, it seems to work out perfectly. Your drive always connects perfectly with that wonderful sounding "wwwwhhhhhhhaaaakkkk" as you watch the ball fly effortlessly up the fairway and onto the green. Your putts are extraordinary, like a giant attractor beam is pulling the ball in the hole regardless of the chosen line (incidentally, whenever I play golf the attractor beam is in every water trap).

I compare this to a great day mountain biking, where no trail is too steep to climb, no stream is too deep to cross, and no roots or other obstacles can reach out and conquer you. Negotiating mountainous terrain with grace and agility on downhill runs that are indescribably steep with just the right mixture of speed, jumps, and switchbacks, you ride like finely tuned machine. This, for me, is euphoria!

The trick to working in your Strength Zone is to first understand what your Strength Zone really is. When you know this, you can adjust your approach to situations (adjust your roles, or your approach to the roles) to take advantage of your Strength Zone. You can do this in many situations, even if it is only for part of the day, when you can shut your office door and work in self-imposed isolation. But in many cases, it doesn't have to be done in isolation, as long as you are able to adjust your approach to the situation appropriately.

However, the real trick to taking advantage of your Strength Zone is not only to know what it is but to sometimes work outside it. That's right, you heard me correctly. The trick to taking advantage of your Strength Zone is to not always work in it! As we discussed previously, one of the goals of personality profiling is to adjust your approach to each situation, to make your communications with others as effective and efficient as possible. Essentially, you are working out of your Strength Zone to ensure that those working with you and around you are working in their Strength Zone.

We can take this principle and apply it to your Overall Strength Zone. For example, assume you have a meeting with a group of people regarding a new product your company is producing. You are responsible for this product and for getting it off the production line on schedule. The people in the meeting are from different areas of the production process. Based on the meeting agenda, you know there are some difficulties in the production process, and each person in the meeting is going to be looking to you for guidance and input into the issues being experienced.

You have the choice to adjust your lenses to your predetermined Strength Zone (to take the disposable camera approach), or you can continually adjust your lenses the way a photographer does when presented with a changing environment. If you chose to leave your lenses focused only on your own Strength Zone, you will severely limit your effectiveness in this meeting because others in the room will rarely adjust their communication style to fit your Strength Zone. This is like a mechanic who assumes every situation can be fixed with a 5/16th wrench, when in most cases it cannot. Sure, in certain situations, the mechanic will be incredibly efficient because he is an absolute expert with a 5/16th wrench, and he can fix anything that this wrench fits. But in the vast majority of situations, the mechanic's effectiveness will be severely limited.

If, instead, you decide to address the situation like the photographer who adjusts his lenses for each unique situation, or like the mechanic who has a complete set of the most up-to-date tools and diagnostic equipment and who understands when and how to apply each of his tools, you will be so much more effective and efficient. In the meeting, you will adjust your lenses appropriately when addressing each person's agenda item and issue.

Your values lens will be adjusted to take into account your company's values, your values, and the values of your co-workers. Maybe one of the issues is schedule constraints that exist because your co-workers want to get off work right at 5 pm to go watch their kids play hockey or football or basketball. If your values lens is adjusted improperly, you may interpret this need to be off work at 5 pm as simple laziness or as a lack of dedication to the company, when this would be entirely wrong. This lack of focus with your values lens could lead to the wrong interpretation of the situation and thus lead you to the wrong conclusion and the wrong solution. The wrong solution could result in failures, both interpersonally and corporately.

Your personality lens needs to be refocused from your personality Strength Zone to the personality Strength Zones of your co-workers. If you are a D, you do not want to communicate as a D if your co-workers are an I, S, or C. In fact, you need to understand what their personality Strength Zone is, so that you can adjust your personality lens to match theirs. In doing this, you will be better able to interpret the data they are giving to you. You will be seeing things from their perspective. You need to communicate through a personality lens that is focused to the personality style of the other person, so that he or she completely understands your point of view.

Your talent lens is the only lens that you should not try to adjust to match another person's style. However, your talent lens does need to be adjusted as the situation dictates. In some cases, you will want to draw upon a particular talent to get the job done, while in other situations, another talent will come to the fore. You also need to understand your talents well enough to know when you are outside your talent area and need to go to someone else who has the appropriate talents to get the job done properly.

Conclusion

Throughout this chapter, we have taken the frayed threads of values, personality, and talents and shown how they are all woven together to form the unique and beautiful tapestry that is you. Identification of this tapestry and understanding its intricacies will allow you to reassess all areas of your life and to realign these areas in a manner that not only better fits you, but allows you to live up to your ultimate potential.

You now should understand how values, personality, and talents all combine to form your Overall Strength Zone and how you can adjust your values, personality, and talents "lenses" to optimize your performance and the performance of those around you in each and every situation and environment.

Summary

1. Complete the values assessment, DISC evaluation, and talent profile.

2. Identify your Overall Strength Zone using the union of sets methodology.

3. Identify your secondary and base strengths.

4. Create a plan to start building on all of these strengths.

5. Begin redefining your role to ensure that you are working in your Strength Zone as much as possible.

Application exercise

1. Take your values, personality profile, and talents and put them into the union of sets diagram below.

2. Take the common traits between values and talents, or talents and personality, or personality and values, and record them in the appropriate circle intersections. These are your secondary strengths, or Secondary Strength Zone. Record them below.

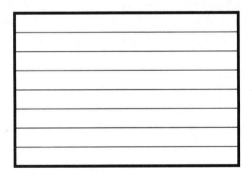

3. Take the values, personality profile traits and talents common to the three circles and write them in the intersection of the three circles. This is your Overall Strength Zone. Record this below.

My Overall Strength Zone is

_____ .

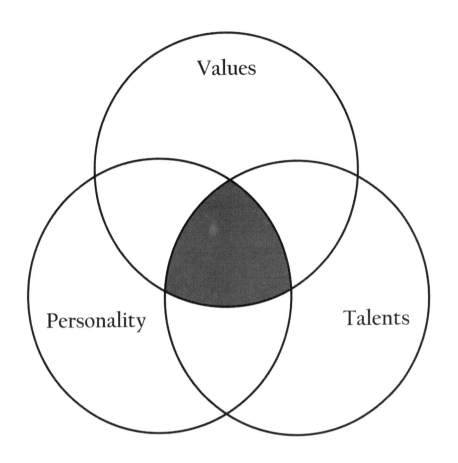

Benefits

·8·

A master in the art of living knows no sharp distinction between his work and his play, his labour and his leisure, his mind and his body, his education and his recreation. He hardly knows which is which. He simply pursues his vision of excellence through whatever he is doing and leaves others to determine whether he is working or playing. To himself he always seems to be doing both.

- George Bernard Shaw

Now that you have discovered how to determine your Strength Zone, what are the benefits of applying the principles taught in this book? How will your life become better when you begin living within your Strength Zone?

When you apply the principles taught in this book, you will achieve a more balanced, highly focused and motivated, less stressed, healthier life. As George Bernard Shaw points out in the above quote, people working in their Strength Zone do not make a distinction between work and play or between education and recreation. In whatever they are doing, they pursue a vision of excellence through their Strength Zone. As a result, they become more successful in all areas of their life.

But what if you don't apply the principles taught in this book to your life? What if you just continue running in the rat race? What could this cost you on a personal level?

We all know that frustration at work causes undue stress. If you are stressed at work, you will typically bring that stress home with you. This can cause marital problems, other family problems, health-related problems, and on and on. It can cause a ripple effect, from you to every person who you come in contact with. On a personal level, the cost can be astronomical.

This reminds me of a story I heard Zig Ziglar tell about little Billy kicking his cat (I've modified and slightly updated the story).

One day at company ABC, the lead salesperson was sitting with the CEO discussing an important but tough-to-crack account. The CEO was stressed because he was falling behind in his work. He was falling behind because he was trying to do too much, and he was not concentrating on what he did well. The salesperson told the CEO that he was afraid that he might lose this important account because of the way things had turned out in a recent meeting.

This was too much for the stressed-out CEO. Instead of offering advice, he exploded into a tirade of threats and belittling. He ended the tirade by declaring that the salesman would lose his job if he lost this important account.

The salesman left the CEO's office outraged. He had worked at ABC for twenty-five years and was the most successful salesperson the company had ever known. That he would lose his job over one lost account was outrageous! How could he be treated like that?

That afternoon, on his way out of the building, he walked past his secretary's office and yelled at her. "If you don't have the paperwork done for my important account by 5 pm this evening, I'll have you fired!"

His secretary could not believe it. She had been his secretary for fifteen years. Everyone knew that his success was due almost entirely to her exemplary service. This was outrageous. She steamed over this the rest of the day as she worked to get the required paperwork completed. As she was leaving the building, she handed the paperwork to the shipping and receiving clerk, saying, "Get this document out as soon as possible. If it does not arrive at its destination by morning I'll personally see to it that you get fired."

Now the shipping and receiving clerk was outraged. This was preposterous, she thought. "I've worked for this company for ten years. If it wasn't for me, this company would have failed years ago. I send packages and receive packages. I ensure that they get to their required destinations on both ends." Steamed, she sent the package and went home to find her son Billy laying on the carpet playing

X-Box. The first thing she noticed was that his jeans were ripped. She tore into him like nothing you have ever seen.

"Billy, I slave all day long for you, and this is how you treat me? Laying on the floor playing video games and ripping your pants. I can't afford to keep buying you video games and new pants. Go to your room and don't come out."

Billy jumped up and muttered under his breath, "This is ridiculous. It's not my fault that I was hit by a car on my way home from school and ripped my pants. It's amazing that I wasn't killed, and all my mom cares about is my pants. Outrageous!"

Just then Billy's cat crossed in front of him. Billy raised his foot and...

As the story illustrates, the results of not working in your Strength Zone can be devastating. All this happened because the CEO was doing too many things and he wasn't able to concentrate on his Strength Zone. This caused him to be stressed and frustrated, and as a result, he set off a chain of negative events. The CEO was not living a balanced, highly focused and motivated, less stressed, healthier life. He was not pursuing his vision of excellence through his Strength Zone in whatever he was doing. He was not seeing success in all areas of his life. This was frustrating him, and his frustration was having a negative impact on many others.

Now change the channel. What would this story look like if the CEO was working in his Strength Zone?

One day at company ABC, the lead salesperson was sitting with the CEO discussing an important but tough-to-crack account. The salesperson told the CEO he was afraid that he might lose this important account because of the way things had turned out in a recent meeting. The CEO began to reassure the salesperson that everything was fine, and they would work together to win the account. The CEO began to work with the salesperson to define the issues and to determine an account strategy. They worked all afternoon, and by the end of the day, they emerged victorious, with a well-defined account strategy. The salesman left the CEO's office excited and motivated. He had worked for ABC Company for twenty-five years and was its most successful salesperson. This new account was going to add to that success. He was pumped. As he walked past his secretary's desk, he complimented her on the paperwork she had prepared for him. He asked her if it was possible to have the paperwork modified as per his meeting with the CEO and to send it over to the prospective client so they would have it first thing in the morning. As he was walking out the door he told her, "With the new strategy that the CEO and I came up with this afternoon. and with your document preparation skills, I just know we are going to land this new account."

His secretary was ecstatic. This would be another important account that she would have the opportunity to help win. She had been with company ABC for fifteen years, and she loved putting these documents together. Her work and track record of winning accounts was exemplary. She was excited and worked hard to produce a great document. When she was completed, she headed to shipping and receiving with the exciting news. "I just know we are going to win this new account. This is going to mean even more profit-sharing for everyone this year, and we get to be part of this. Can I get you to send this document to the prospective client right away, so they will have it first thing in the morning?"

Now the shipping and receiving clerk was excited. If we win this account, we will get more profit sharing, she thought, and I definitely need that. I love being responsible for getting these documents to our clients. I have worked for this company for ten years, and the documents have never been late, even if it meant I had to carry them myself. After sending the package, she went home to find her son Billy laying on the carpet playing X-Box. The first thing she noticed was that his jeans were ripped.

"Billy, what happened to your pants?" she asked.

Billy jumped up. "Mom, you wouldn't believe it. I was on my way home from school, and a car ran the stop sign as I was crossing the street. Its back bumper caught my jeans and pulled me so hard that I fell down. All of my friends started yelling, but I was okay, except for my ripped jeans."

"Oh my goodness, Billy!" said his mom. "Are you sure you're okay? Come over here and let me see you." She gave him a huge hug, saying, "I'm so glad you aren't hurt. I love you so much!"

Just then Billy's cat crossed in front of him. He reached down, picked up the cat, and gave it a hug.

What a difference in outcomes! All because the CEO was working in is Strength Zone and able to use his strengths to help the worried salesperson, building his confidence and positively affecting the lives of at least three other people (and a cat).

Financial

According to the research done by Brian Tracy in his Success Mastery Academy seminar, each year of education is equal to $200,000 over the course of a lifespan. Tracy explains that, on average, people with high school diplomas will earn about $600,000 over their lifetime. People with two-year college degrees will earn an additional $400,000 or a total of $1 million over their lifetime. Likewise, people with four-year degrees will earn $1.4 million, and people with six-year masters degrees will earn $1.8 million. Note that these numbers are a few years old and have not been adjusted for inflation. The point, however, remains valid – the more education you get, the more earning capacity you have.

Now consider this: if you customize your education so that you concentrate on your Strength Zone, and if you continually work at building yourself into a tower of strength within your Strength Zone through a process of targeted education, I believe that your potential to achieve wealth is absolutely unlimited!

Business

Businesses benefit in many ways by following the concepts taught in *Strength Zone*. One of the major benefits is in recruiting. As most people know, recruiting can cost a lot of money. If the wrong person is hired, it can cost the organization a lot more. Based on my experience, it can cost between $10,000 and $100,000 to recruit and hire a qualified individual. The price typically increases as the industry experience requirement increases.

By applying the principles taught in *Strength Zone*, I have found that we are able to hire people quicker, and we have a higher success ratio when integrating these new hires into our team.

When we interview people, we listen intently, striving to determine the basic personality profile of the candidate during the interview. We ask them questions about their values and try to determine their talents. We use this information to ensure that we do not hire people whose personality, values, and talents do not fit those of the rest of the team.

For example, we recently interviewed a candidate who was technically sound, but his personality was not a fit for the rest of the team. He had an S-C type of personality, which, if you recall from our personality training, is a person that is a very steady performer, detail oriented, avoids stress, and dislikes change. We were hiring for a demanding position in a fast-paced environment that was full of change. Through the interview process, we were able to determine that in this environment, he would have been eaten alive by his co-workers and by the client. Consequently, we did not hire him but went with another more suitable candidate. Had we hired this individual, we would have sunk thousands of dollars into getting him up to speed with our processes and procedures and getting him mobilized overseas in our construction yards. We then would have spent more money trying to coach and cajole him along to success, only to probable failure in the end. I estimate that if we would have made this mistake, it would have cost us at least $50,000 in training and mobilization. It potentially would have cost us with our client as well. The last thing any company wants is to fail in front of its client. This could be disastrous. It could cost anything from an embarrassment to losing the client altogether. For us, losing this particular client would have meant $52 million in lost annual revenue.

I have also found that we are able to retain existing employees because we pay more attention to their needs, values, strengths, and passions. It is much cheaper in the long term to treat employees properly by placing them in roles that allow them to work in their Strength Zone than it is to lose and replace them. However, no matter how hard you try to be proactive, there will always be cases where a key employee feels that it is time to move on. If that employee is in a key role, it can be very costly. When it happens, the first thing you must do is determine if the employee was truly working in his or her Strength Zone. Were the employee's values frequently violated? Were there consistent personality clashes with others? Were the talents of that employee not being properly utilized? Asking these questions directly can lead to some enlightening answers. In many cases, the answers point to the reason the person has decided to leave. If you can pinpoint the issue, you may have an opportunity to save the individual.

In one case, we had an employee who was integral to our team. To lose him would have jeopardized many of our relationships with one client and could have given us a black eye with that client. When he called me out of the blue on a Friday afternoon to let me know he was giving his two-week notice, I was shocked and dazed. I asked him the standard questions: "When is your last day?" and "Why are you leaving?" I got the standard answers: "In two weeks," and "For better opportunities."

I convinced the individual not to officially accept his new position until I had an opportunity to think about his situation and to respond appropriately. I then took the evening to review his past and current roles and to build some questions for him. After doing this review, I realized we might not have been utilizing him in his Strength Zone. On Saturday, I called him and began to ask questions around his values and talents. While there were no issues from a personality standpoint, it quickly became apparent that some of his values were being violated, and he felt he was not being used in a way that took advantage of his talents. I asked him if he would stay if we could address the issues. He said yes and gave me until Monday to come up with some changes that would take care of the issues he identified. I worked through the weekend and was able to come up with a solution that allowed this individual to move back into his Strength Zone from both a values and talents perspective.

Some people might say that if someone has decided to leave a company, you should just let him or her go. I agree with this if the only issue is compensation. However, if the person is leaving because of not being used properly, then the fault should lie with corporate leadership. If this person is valued, it is much better if you can convince him or her to stay and then pick up your socks as a management team by placing this person in a position that takes advantage of his or her Strength Zone.

Incidentally, saving this person from leaving our company saved us at least $100,000 in recruiting costs, unproductive training time, and other related issues. This does not take into account any losses we could have incurred due to our client losing confidence in us.

What about the day-to-day interactions? Improvement in this area can save literally thousands of dollars. For example, let's take a look at a typical day for Sam, an employee, in a project environment. In a day,

Sam will have many interactions with many different people. However, for arguments sake, let's say that Sam has ten interactions that involve discussing some aspect of the project, or some deliverable, or a requirement of some sort. This could be a commitment from Sam to the other person or from the other person back to Sam. Depending on the level of complexity, these interactions can last for quite some time. Again, for arguments sake, assume that each interaction lasts for thirty minutes. Now assume that Sam is well aware of his own Strength Zone and that he has knowledge of his co-worker's Strength Zone. He uses this knowledge to better understand his co-worker's message to him. He adjusts his response to the co-worker in a way that helps them interact more quickly and efficiently. Assume that Sam, working in this way, is able to shave ten minutes off each interaction by avoiding a prolonged discussion and by avoiding a second meeting for clarification.

Ten minutes is one-sixth of an hour, which is 0.167 hours per interaction. Assume that you have fifty people in your area of influence, and all fifty people have taken the same training as Sam. Your savings are 0.167 hours per interaction, multiplied by ten interactions a day, multiplied by fifty people, equals 83.3 hours per day. If the overhead cost in this group is $50 per hour, you are saving 83.3 hours per day times $50 per hour equals $4,166.67 per day. This might not seem like much when you are running multimillion-dollar projects, but consider that there are 260 workdays in a year. Your savings are $4,166.67 times 260 equals $1,083,333 per year. This is nothing to sneeze at! Assuming you provide four hours of training per year per employee to keep everyone up to date on these principles, your ROI equals an amazing 10,733 percent. Amazing! (See the activity at the end of this chapter for th detailed ROI calculation).

What is even more amazing is that this investment will pay for it with only a $77 per day improvement. This is a 1.5 hours-per improvement split between fifty people or about two mir improvement per day per person.

In addition to these amazing savings and return on investmen does an unmotivated and unfocused workforce cost an em believe the cost is enormous. Just look at simple things that are in our workforce today. Things like:

- Simple inefficiency on the job – according to some statistics, only thirty percent of North American employees feel they are producing at peak levels. This is huge – seventy percent of our workers feel that they are wrongly deployed and could be producing more than they are now.

- De-motivation, apathy, and general lack of drive

- An increase in unwarranted sick days – if each employee takes one sick day a year just because they don't feel like coming into work and you have fifty employees with an average hourly cost of $50 per hour, this costs your company $20,000 per year.

- An increase in employee errors that require rework or result in off-spec products – the financial cost can be huge if the product is wasted, if rework is required, and if the production or supply chain is impacted.

- Lower production rates

- Increased stress in the workplace

- Increase in health care costs due to increased stress

- Increase in time spent doing non-business-related activities during work hours (personal email, personal phone calls, Internet browsing, non-business-related conversations). There are a number of estimates out there on average time wasted by employees, and I'm not sure that a general consensus has been reached. However, being conservative, I think we can estimate that each unmotivated employee wastes approximately half an hour in an eight-hour day. This time is wasted because the employee is bored, unchallenged, and not working in his or her Strength Zone. If you have fifty such employees at $50 per hour wasting a half hour per day, this is costing your company $325,000 per year.

Many of these problems can be avoided by providing some basic training to help your employees and their managers understand their Strength Zone and redefine their roles or find new roles that take advantage of this Strength Zone. This will ultimately lead to more satisfaction in the workplace and will be a big factor in increasing the thirty percent of employees who feel they are producing at peak levels to a number closer to one hundred percent.

Internal corporate communication

Another area where I believe poor application of Strength Zones is costing corporations a lot of money is in reporting from the lower echelons to upper management. It is here where some of the biggest disconnects and largest oversights appear in a corporation. The lower echelons always seem to know if a new (or existing) product is working in the marketplace. They have ideas on how to improve it, and they can often explain how a competitor's product may be better. In most organizations, however, not a lot of effort is put into these communications. As a result, products are not as good as they could be, and corporations lose market share.

A good example of this is the dramatic decrease in popularity of the Barbie doll between 2001 and 2004. During this period, Mattel lost twenty percent of its share of the doll market to other companies that were taking advantage of the latest trend – dolls modeled after celebrities. I find it hard to believe that no one in Mattel saw this coming. Maybe no one in management, but I am convinced that many of Mattel's employees were being hounded by their kids for celebrity dolls. Why wasn't this communicated to management?

Another example was the introduction of low-calorie beer by a well-known American beer company in September 2002. By March 2004, the brewer was the market leader, capturing 5.7 percent of the light beer market with its signature brand. Why didn't its closest competitor catch on to this? The competitor didn't launch its low-calorie product until March 2004, and by then, it was too late. Their sales climbed to 0.4 percent of the market by July and then began sliding. I find it hard to believe that there were not any health-conscious people within the competing organization looking for a low-calorie beer. Why was this need not communicated to upper management?

There isn't a simple answer to this question. Many factors play into the failure to act, or to act quicker than the competition, including a lack of corporate peripheral vision as outlined in the November 2005 edition of the Harvard Business Review, which is where the statistics for these two examples came from. I believe that a workforce trained to understand Strength Zones, both theirs and others, would have a substantially better chance at communicating their concerns and ideas upward. I also believe that management would have a better chance of understanding what was being communicated if they, too, were trained to understand Strength Zones.

If this communication had taken place at both the toy manufacturer and the brewing company, the loss of market share either would not have happened or it would certainly not have been as severe.

Strength Zone files

One of the practical things I do to ensure that key employees are working within their Strength Zone is to create a profile for each employee. Each profile includes a DISC evaluation, the person's top six values and the top five talents defined by StrengthsFinder.com. I take these three things and summarize the employee's performance and preferences into a few brief paragraphs.

What this profiling exercise does is identify how the employee prefers to work and where he or she can perform the best. For example, I have project managers that are all highly competent individuals and capable of managing complex projects, but they all have distinct areas where they perform extremely well and other areas where they don't do well at all. It is up to me to know this and to ensure that I am setting them up for success. Incidentally, it is probably a good exercise to build a profile for yourself first and have others review it for accuracy before proceeding to build profiles on your employees.

Take a look at these three project manager profiles:

Mr. X
Personality Style – D-C
Talents – Learner, Responsibility, Achiever, Belief, Self-Assurance
Values – Faith/Religion, Family, Accountable, Honesty, Integrity, Trust

Summary – Mr. X is able to handle an extreme workload in a demanding and changing environment. He seems to thrive under pressure. He can juggle multiple projects and is very detail-oriented. He takes a hands-on approach to his projects. Not much gets past Mr. X. He has control of most aspects of his projects from contracts and budgets down to execution. He is process-oriented. With his home in central U.S., Mr. X will and does travel extensively and will go on the road for weeks or months at a time. Although he does not go looking for high-conflict situations, Mr. X will not avoid them, and he is adept at working his way through them. He has managed projects valued up to $9 million U.S.

Mr. X can be very blunt and has been perceived as abrasive. However, he has been improving in this area over the last few years. Having said that, this type of personality is what is required when dealing with the international engineering contractors, especially when our contract is with an EPC (company that does engineering, procurement, and construction). Mr. X is effective as a manager on EPC contracts. Mr. X manages the contract and does not back down.

Mr. Y
Personality Style – D-C
Talents – Command, Competition, Maximizer, Significance, and Activator
Values – Accountable, Authority, Commit, Competition, Growth, Perfection

Summary – Mr. Y is able to handle an extreme workload in a demanding and changing environment. He is able to juggle multiple projects but is not very detail oriented. He takes a hands-off approach to project management and requires other members of his team to be on top of the details. He is process-oriented and expects everyone working for him to follow the processes in place. Mr. Y can be blunt under pressure but is typically diplomatic and professional. Although he does not go looking for high-conflict situations, Mr. Y will not avoid them and is adept at working his way through them. He has managed projects in excess of $60 million U.S.

Mr. Y has a wealth of experience in offshore oil and gas. He has leveraged this experience and has been vital in building our current relationship with our client. Mr. Y has strong interpersonal skills and has built one-on-one relationships with key individuals within our client's organization.

Although Mr. Y has traveled extensively over the last five years, he has expressed a desire to remain closer to home without any long-term rotations in the future.

Mr. Z
Personality Style – S-C
Talents – Ideation, Significance, Futuristic, Intellection, Analytical
Values – Change, Creativity, Happiness, Integrity, Self-Respect, Wisdom

Summary – Mr. Z is able to handle a moderate workload. This workload has, at times, spiked up to a large workload, and he was able to handle it, but this situation does seem to cause Mr. Z undue stress. He does not thrive under large workloads and is adverse to extreme amounts of change. Mr. Z is a detail-oriented project manager with respect to finances and contracts, but he takes a more hands-off approach on the technical execution. He has handled projects up to $19 million U.S.

Mr. Z avoids high-conflict situations. Although Mr. Z is willing to travel, he is not willing to rotate long-term unless he can turn the rotation into a relocation for him and his family.

These project managers are all highly regarded and do excellent work. However, if I were to switch projects between Mr. X and Mr. Z, we would start to see some problems. Mr. X would end up getting bored and would probably look for another job. Mr. Z would be overwhelmed with the change, conflict, and contract management and would experience some dramatic failures. We would see the same issues if we switched projects between Mr. Y and Mr. Z, as Mr. X is quite similar to Mr. Y.

The difference between Mr. X and Mr. Y is more subtle. They are both capable project managers who can handle large projects, lots of change, and lots of stress. However, the difference that could cause problems is in two main areas:

1. Mr. Y does not want to travel much anymore. He needs a project that allows him to be close to his home base, not a project that requires him to rotate or travel continually. Mr. X does not have these constraints.

2. Mr. X gets into the details of project execution, but Mr. Y does not. If we were to give Mr. Y technically weaker team members, his project may fail because he does not manage at that level. Mr. X does, and as a result, it is much better to place new hires or more junior technical staff with him, as he provides detailed checks and mentoring throughout the project.

These individual traits are not bad things. It is this uniqueness between individuals that provides options to management as the leadership makes strategic decisions in running the business. Conversely, if management does not understand its people and their Strength Zones, it is this same uniqueness that can cause dramatic failures within an organization.

Application exercise

1. Calculate your ROI for training your employees similar to the example given with Sam on page 200 and 201.

E = # of employees _____

I = # of interactions per day per employee _____

N = # of employees_____

T = Time savings per interaction in hours _____

C = Average overhead cost per hour of employees _____

W = # of workdays in a year _____

Tr = hours of training per employee_____

ROI = [(T * I * N *C*W) – (E * C * Tr)] / (E * C * Tr) * 100

ROI = _____

2. Create an employee profile similar to those shown on pages 204, 205 and 206 for those who work for you.

Mr./Mrs./Ms. _____

Personality Style –

Talents –

Values –

Summary – Mr./Mrs./Ms. _____ is _____

_____

_____

_____

_____

Conclusion

· 9 ·

One can choose to go back toward safety or forward toward growth. Growth must be chosen again and again; fear must be overcome again and again.

- Abraham Maslow

Great minds have purposes, others have wishes.

- Washington Irving

You are not here merely to make a living. You are here in order to enable the world to live more amply, with greater vision, with a finer spirit of hope and achievement. You are here to enrich the world, and you impoverish yourself if you forget the errand.

- Woodrow Wilson

So what is your choice?

Will you run from your fears and head back toward safety? Will you stick with wishes rather than purpose, and exist only to make a living? Will you put down this book and go on living the same life you always have?

Or will you choose to go forward toward growth, to overcome your fears, find your purpose, and enable the world to live more amply with greater vision, with a finer spirit of hope and achievement? Will you pick up this book again and again, learning the principles being taught and applying them to your life?

My hope is that you will choose the latter course of action and that you would find that place where something in your heart would say, "This is what I was made for!"

I believe that finding your Strength Zone is the first step in this direction. By finding your Strength Zone and striving to work and live within it, you are choosing to move forward toward growth. You are heading into unknown territory, moving away from the known and comfortable and taking your fears head on. You are striving through your Strength Zone to find your purpose, and then through this process, you can work with others to help them do the same. Collectively, those of us who are on this path can enable the world to live more amply with greater vision and in a finer spirit of hope and achievement.

This certainly sounds a whole lot more exciting and fulfilling than putting this book down and going back to running from your fears and merely existing.

Through this book, we have learned some simple – yet profound – principles regarding ourselves and how we interact with the world around us. How our values, personalities, and talents play into our overall success as individuals in each and every one of the many roles that we have in life. We have learned how we can increase our effectiveness by at least one hundred percent just by beginning to work in our Strength Zone more often and in more of our roles. We also know that this increase in effectiveness does not have to be limited to one hundred percent. If we really make a concerted effort to rearrange our roles to take advantage of our Strength Zone, the resultant increase in effectiveness can be unlimited.

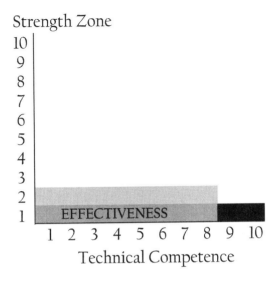

We have also learned how to take this Strength Zone process to those around us, increasing their effectiveness. When these people do the same with those around them, we will see their effectiveness increase in a pyramid effect that flows back up to us in multiplied or even exponential effectiveness increases.

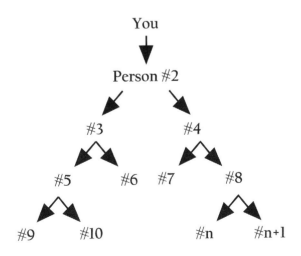

So how did we arrive at our Overall Strength Zone? We determined our Values Strength Zone, Personality Strength Zone, and Talents Strength Zone. We then looked at the intersection between these three seemingly distinct zones and determined the overlap between them. This overlap is our Overall Strength Zone. It is up to each of us to always review our roles in every area of life to determine how best to work within our Strength Zone in each one of these roles. I have developed a Statement of Purpose for values, personality, and talents that will help remind you of what we are trying to achieve with this process.

Values: I will strive to work and live within my values and to ensure that I will never violate any of my values for any reason. I will be understanding and respectful of the values of others and of my corporation, and I will endeavor to align their values with my own (without violating any values) in order to work in harmony with others.

Personality: I will make every effort to communicate to everyone in the most efficient method possible. I will strive to keep my personality balanced appropriately so that I continually exhibit positive personality traits and I will work to foster positive and productive relationships with others.

Talents: I will strive to work within my areas of greatest talent, and I will always work to build these talent areas into towers of strength and increase my personal effectiveness. I will not worry about areas that I am not talented in unless they become areas of weakness that could affect my performance, and then I will strive to move someone with strengths into these weakness areas.

My challenge to you as we close this book is this: Do not live your life desperately trying to avoid failure. Do not languish in agonized mediocrity. My challenge is that you live your life confident enough to embrace failure by using what you learn from each failure as a stepping stone to success. Shun the urge to run from fear and always move towards growth. I challenge you to break free from mediocrity and enjoy a life flourishing in unimagined excellence!

Finding your Strength Zone is the first step in fulfilling this challenge. What you do with this Strength Zone knowledge will determine your level of unimagined excellence!

Recommended Reading

This list is available for download at
www.StrengthZone.ca:

Personal Development:
- Power of Focus by Les Hewitt, Jack Canfield and Mark Victor Hansen
- Now, Discover Your Strengths by Donald Clifton and Marcus Buckingham
- The 5 Faces of Genius by Annette Moser-Wellman
- Life is a Series of Presentations by Tony Jeary
- Thinking for a Change by John C. Maxwell
- Today Matters by John C. Maxwell
- The Magic of Thinking Big by David J. Schwartz
- Top Performance by Zig Ziglar
- As A Man Thinketh by James Allen
- Successful Intelligence by Robert J. Sternberg
- The Power of Positive Thinking by Norman Vincent Peale
- Move Ahead with Possibility Thinking by Robert Schuller
- The Present by Spencer Johnson
- Who Moved my Cheese by Spencer Johnson
- The Seven Habits of Highly Effective People by Steven Covey
- Psychology of Winning by Dennis Waitley
- Man's Search for Meaning by Viktor E. Frankl
- How to Win Friends and Influence People by Dale Carnegie
- Winning with People by John C. Maxwell
- Time Traps by Todd Duncan
- Never Eat Alone by Keith Ferrazzi

Leadership:
- The 21 Irrefutable Laws of Leadership by John C. Maxwell

- Courageous Leadership by Bill Hybels
- Developing the Leader Within You by John C. Maxwell
- The One Minute Manager by Kenneth Blanchard and Spencer Johnsen
- Fish Tales by Stephen C. Lundin and John Christensen and Harry Paul
- Death by Meeting by Patrick Lencioni
- The Five Temptations of a CEO by Patrick Lencioni
- Who Says Elephants Can't Dance? by Louis V. Gerstner Jr.
- The 17 Indisputable Laws of Teamwork by John C. Maxwell
- Leaders by Warren Bennis and Burt Nanus
- The Leadership Challenge by Kouzes and Posner

Management:
- The Heart of Change by John P. Kotter
- The Effective Executive by Peter F. Drucker
- Good To Great by Jim Collins
- Managing With Carrots by Adrian Gostick and Chester Elton

Financial/Economic/Business:
- Unlimited Wealth by Paul Zane Pilzer
- Mastering The Rockfeller Habits by Verne Harnish
- The Five Rituals of Wealth by Tod Barnhart
- Multiple Streams of Income by Robert G. Allen
- The Millionare Mind by Thomas J. Stanley
- Guide to Investing by Robert T. Kiyosaki
- The Emyth by Michael Gerber

Biographies:
- Jack, Straight From the Gut by Jack Welch
- Leadership by Rudolph W. Giuliani
- My American Journey by Colin Powell

Religious/Faith
- Purpose Driven Life by Rick Warren
- The Dream Giver by Bruce Wilkinson
- Epic by John Eldredge
- Waking the Dead by John Eldredge
- Running With The Giants by John C. Maxwell
- Mere Christianity by CS Lewis

Recommended Resources

· Appendix B ·

- www.StrengthZone.ca

- The Power of Focus. www.thepoweroffocus.ca

- Key Principles Self Evaluation: Development Dimensions International. www.ddiworld.com

- Interaction Guidelines: Development Dimensions International. www.ddiworld.com

- Leadership Practices Inventory: www.pfeiffer.com (1-800-274-4434)

- Managing by Motivation by Marshal Sashkin. www.hrdpress.com (1-800-822-2801)

- Leadership Process: Motivating Achievement. Spencer, Shenk, Capers & Associates, Inc. (1-310-515-7555)

- DISC Insights Personality System: The Institute for Motivational Living, Inc. www.discinsights.com

- www.myersbriggs.org/

About the Author

A graduate from the University of Alberta in 1989 with a B.Sc. in Electrical Engineering, David M. Taylor is a professional engineer with sixteen years of electrical engineering and project management experience. Over the past ten years, he has held project management and leadership roles, working with management and staff to improve overall performance in the development and implementation of business and project execution standards. Some of the industries he has served are: chemical and petrochemical manufacturing, conventional oil and gas production, heavy and synthetic oil production and upgrading, gas and liquids processing, environmental protection and offshore oil and gas production.

David has invested a lot of time into his own personal development, as well as that of his staff. He has learned a tremendous amount about placing people in roles that allow them to capitalize on their strengths. While much of this learning experience has been in the form of courses, seminars, and other studies, it has all been proven through real-life application. He has learned through failures and successes. **Strength Zone** is a summary of the system he currently uses to train leaders and project managers to take advantage of their strengths and the strengths of those who work with and for them.

David is a member of the Association of Professional Engineers, Geologists, and Geophysicists of Alberta (APEGGA). He lives in Calgary, Alberta and spends his spare time with his family at their summer cottage in Sylvan Lake as well as mountain biking, climbing, and fishing with his son Drew.